Learning for Life

A programme for young people

Ken Longman

Macmillan Education

© Ken Longman 1981

First published 1981
Reprinted 1982 (twice)

Published by
MACMILLAN EDUCATION LTD
Houndmills Basingstoke Hampshire RG21 2XS
and London
Associated companies throughout the world

Printed in Hong Kong

Cartoons by Lorraine Calaora

British Library Cataloguing in Publication Data

Longman, Ken
Learning for life.
1. Vocational guidance - Great Britain
I. Title
331.7'02'0941   HF5382.5.G7

ISBN 0-333-27656-6

Contents

Our world today – your world tomorrow

Acknowledgements

The author and publishers wish to thank the following who have kindly given permission for the use of copyright material:

London Express News and Feature Services for an extract 'The Strong Man They Call Maria' by John Morgan from the *Daily Express*, 1978; Times Newspapers Limited for an article 'Simple Sums Floor Vast Majority of Pupils' by David Nicholson-Lord in *The Times Educational Supplement*, March 1978; Trades Union Congress for an extract from *Going to Work: A Short Guide to Trade Unionism*.

The author also wishes to thank the Distributive Industries Training Board, the Engineering ITB and the Rubber and Plastics ITB for their co-operation.

Every effort has been made to trace all the copyright holders, but if any have been inadvertently overlooked the publishers will be pleased to make the necessary arrangement at the first opportunity.

The author and publishers wish to acknowledge the following photograph sources:

British Hovercraft Corporation Ltd. p. 27 bottom left.   British Petroleum p. 27 top.   Commissioner of Police of the Metropolis p. 11 bottom.   Crown copyright - Dept. of Health & Social Security p. 92 top.   Courtesy of British Aerospace, Hatfield p. 27 bottom left.   Engineering Careers Information Service p. 35.   Richard & Sally Greenhill pp. 19 bottom, 61 top, 92 bottom.   Manpower Services Commission - Bill Colman pp. 11 top, 31.   Marks & Spencer Ltd. p. 32.   Midland Group Services Ltd. p. 1.   Rubber & Plastics Industry Training Board pp. 19 top, 61 bottom left and right, 75, 76, 85.   Janine Wiedel p. 20.

Every effort has been made to trace all the copyright holders but if any have been inadvertently overlooked the publishers will be pleased to make the necessary arrangement at the first opportunity.

Our world today -
Your world tomorrow

Every human being can think ahead.
Animals cannot; they live entirely in the
present. For small children, too, the period
from one Saturday to the next is a very
long time – and a skilful parent can easily
bring about changes in their immediate
attention. (Think of some examples you
have seen of this.) But you can not only
think about the future; you can shape your
own as well.

You are living in an age when workers,
and students including yourselves, are
likely to have more leisure. It is important
for your own satisfaction that you spend it
in a way that is rewarding both to
yourselves and possibly to others less
fortunate than you. But you are also
entering or involved in a world of work
which is becoming increasingly technical.
New jobs are emerging, new skills are
required, new chances and opportunities
are arising.

In both leisure and work you should
decide what you will become so good at
that it could be regarded as your 'personal
excellence'. There will be many
opportunities for you to develop yourself

as a worker, as an individual, and as a
member of the community in which you
live.

Young people like yourselves can turn
many situations to your advantage - if only
you know how. In becoming a worker, you
need to
a) recognise what role you want for
yourself, and know how to achieve it;
b) be aware of the qualifications you need
in order to enter work, further education
and training;
c) discover what prospects there are for
you in your chosen job;
d) anticipate what barriers and new
opportunities exist to hinder and help you.

Decide what you want for yourself

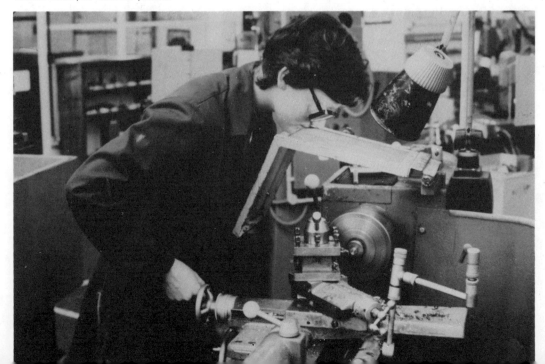

An example of these new opportunities

The courses set up by the Technical Education Council (TEC) and Business Education Council (BEC) do not always demand minimum attainment. Opportunities exist for all young people. Youth Opportunity Programmes and Unified Vocational Preparation (UVP) courses provide a means of becoming successful both before work and in work. Consult your careers teacher, tutor, local careers office and colleges of further education to find out about opportunities such as these.

Possible routes

Many jobs have an easily recognised and understood method of entry; for example, a) to become a technician, you leave school at sixteen having gained the necessary qualifications, you get a job as an apprentice technician and you follow a day- or block-release course at a college of further education;
b) to become a successful shop worker you get a job, show you are good at it and seek further training. If your employer cannot provide that, you could enrol on your own at a college of further education and follow, for example, a course leading to a Distribution Certificate, awarded by the Distributive Industry Training Board (DITB).

It is sometimes more difficult to see how to obtain a job and/or qualification. To help examine things more clearly it can be useful to design an algorithm, or pathway. Below is an amusing algorithm of how to obtain a drink without actually paying for it.

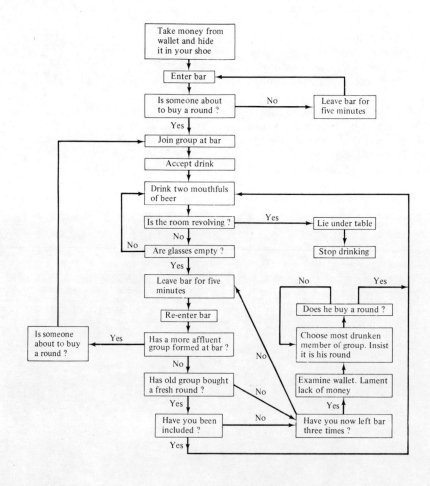

An example of an algorithm for working out how to get a particular job is as follows:

I wish to become a mechanic. How can I do so?

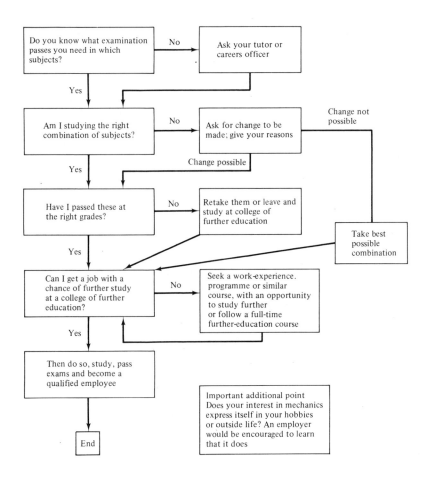

Now design your own algorithm for a person who wants to become a hairdresser, or for your personal career interest.

Choosing

It is important to make the right choice at each stage. No choice is totally disastrous; but quite serious mistakes can occur, and increase the difficulty of achieving your ambitions - for example, if the wrong selection is made at 13+, or when first seeking work. Choosing wisely can prevent you going down blind alleys. When making a choice you should not be influenced by the preferences of others - but do listen carefully to your tutor, parents and friends.

Learn to select the information and advice which suits your own needs. Of course, you must know those needs before you can do that!

This is your life

The purpose of this book is to help you to understand what kind of person you are, and to decide what kind of person you hope to become, what kind of work you would like to do and what kind of life you

Understand what kind of person you hope to become

would like to lead. A child of four may want to become a train driver - but he or she will have no idea of the skills needed. Such an ambition is a fantasy. Towards the middle and end of your school career we hope that you will be able to make your dreams come true; but dreams do not come true on their own. Are you prepared to make the necessary effort? Work with your tutor, and the author, so that between us we will help:

you as an individual

a) to understand yourself better;
b) to make better decisions;

you as a worker

c) to know what possibilities exist;
d) to know how to get where you want to go in your job and life-style;

you as a member of your community

e) to understand others and their needs;
f) to find a satisfying place in your community;
g) to explore all possibilities;
h) to decide what kind of world you want.

A task for you

Find out the name and address of your nearest college of further education. Send for its syllabuses, and with a group of friends find out from the syllabuses what courses would meet your interests or help your leisure activities. How could you enrol and participate in these? If your tutor is too busy, organise for yourself a group visit to the college.

Find out from your tutor, or from the college, the addresses of the Technical Education Council (TEC) and Business Education Council (BEC). Ask what opportunities there are for improving the employability of young people a) before they find work, and b) after they have found work – your local careers office should be able to help you, too, or your nearest Youth Opportunities Programme office.

Find out from your local library or Citizens Advice Bureau what opportunities there are for you to follow such leisure activities and interests as fishing, painting, interior decorating, judo – in fact, whatever you fancy.

4

Unit I **This is you**

1.1 Personal details

In a job it is very important not only that you should have the right qualifications and training to enable you to do it well, but also that the work and working conditions should suit your personality. So you have to know yourself well in the first place. Other factors, too, such as the jobs your parents and close friends do, will colour the way you think about work.

In the exercise which follows, all the answers may affect your career plans. For example, some people have the type of skin condition which will not allow them to handle food or certain materials, e.g. glass fibre.

Exercise 1a

Copy out the form below and fill it in carefully. It may be collected by your tutor and later used for guidance in your interview with your careers officer.

Name		Form	Age	Yrs	Mths
Address			Tel. No.		
Father's occupation		Mother's occupation			
Previous secondary school(s) attended	1		Dates attended	1	
	2			2	
School subjects	Level (O; CSE; not decided; 16 + ; or no exam)		Subjects you *like* best	Subjects you *do* best	

Is your health good?				
Do you want to tell your careers teacher of any health problems?				
Teams, clubs, societies (include offices such as prefects, etc.)				
Hobbies, interests, pastimes, clubs, etc.				
Name up to 3 jobs you would quite like to do				
Name up to 3 jobs you believe you would hate				
Your timetable (please include room numbers where possible):				
Monday	Tuesday	Wednesday	Thursday	Friday

Exercise 1b

Write an introduction to yourself, including all aspects you think are important. This account will only be read by your tutor, and your friends if you choose.

1.2 Knowing yourself

How well do you really know yourself? What is your opinion of yourself? Does it match other people's opinion of you or not? Or do you not know? Why not try it and see?

Exercise 2

Copy out the table below and place a tick in the Yes or No column according to whether each statement is true or not for you as you see yourself. Mark this one out of twenty-five under the guidance of your tutor.

Personality	Yes No
I would rather be someone else	
There are not many things I like about myself	
I am fun to be with	
I am slow at learning new things	
I have more difficulties than most people	
I am a moody and confused person	
I succeed at most tasks I attempt	
Many other people are more attractive than me	
I am not easily upset	
I am trustworthy and reliable	

Behaviour	
I work hard	
I make up my mind quickly	
I do not stand up for myself	
I speak my mind	
I would like to leave home as soon as possible	

Relationships	
I disagree with my parents on most issues	
People usually like me very much	

	Yes No
I cannot easily talk to a group of people	
People want too much from me	
I am a better team leader than team member	
I can talk things over with my parents	
I am not well liked by people of my own age	
My parents are understanding and fair	
People at school or work often make me angry	
My parents boss me about without regard to my feelings	

Do others see you as you see yourself?

1.3 How do you see yourself? How do others see you?

There are really three yous – you as you see yourself, you as others see you, and you as you really are. You can find out about the first two fairly easily, but to get to know the real you is far more difficult.

Exercise 3

Copy out the table in the left-hand column of the next page and tick each item *honestly* in what you feel is the correct column for yourself. Then ask a close friend to draw circles in the columns as she or he sees you. How do those answers agree or disagree with your own view of yourself?

This is the way I am: How I see myself.
(There are no right or wrong answers, only honest ones.)

I am	nearly always	half the time	just now and then
friendly	————	————	————
obedient	————	————	————
honest	————	————	————
thoughtful	————	————	————
brave	————	————	————
careful	————	————	————
fair	————	————	————
mean	————	————	————
lazy	————	————	————
truthful	————	————	————
smart	————	————	————
polite	————	————	————
clean	————	————	————
kind	————	————	————
selfish	————	————	————
a nuisance	————	————	————
neat	————	————	————
a help at home	————	————	————
good at art	————	————	————
conscientious	————	————	————
scared to take chances	————	————	————
helpful	————	————	————
co-operative	————	————	————
cheerful	————	————	————
jealous	————	————	————
sincere	————	————	————
studious	————	————	————
loyal	————	————	————
likeable	————	————	————
a good sport	————	————	————
useful	————	————	————
dependable	————	————	————
shy	————	————	————
happy	————	————	————
popular	————	————	————
nervous	————	————	————
sad	————	————	————
nice-looking	————	————	————
optimistic	————	————	————
as lucky as others	————	————	————
good at making things	————	————	————

Exercise 4

Under your tutor's guidance, form groups of three or four. Each group will make a list of two or three jobs which require each of the following: patience, firmness, tact, honesty, energy, strength, manual skill, above-average height, no colour-blindness, neat personal appearance, an outgoing nature, years of study, little or no study, ability to supervise others, working alone, working in a team.

1.4 Work priorities

So far you have looked at yourself and the kind of person you are. Now it is time to think about yourself in relation to work.

Exercise 5

Make a copy of the exercise below and overleaf. In the left-hand column of lines tick the five (and *only* five) factors to which you attach most importance. Then, in the right-hand column, write the order of importance to *you* of these factors; for example, if you have ticked 'working near home' in the left-hand column and it is the most important to you of the five, write '1' against it in the right-hand column.

Time at work
regular hours —— ——
a five-day week —— ——
no shiftwork —— ——
no weekend work —— ——
flexitime —— ——

Payment
high wages —— ——
plenty of tips —— ——
subsidised meals —— ——

Company
working with lots of people —— ——
working with your own age group —— ——
working with people of your own sex —— ——
working with people of the
    opposite sex —— ——
working on your own —— ——
working in a team —— ——

(cont.)

Conditions

a chance to drive	——	——
a chance to travel	——	——
a variety of jobs to do	——	——
working near home	——	——
light, airy working conditions	——	——
opportunities to meet the public	——	——
working in a large firm	——	——
sports and social clubs	——	——
transport provided to and from work	——	——

Status

being able to supervise others	——	——
a chance for further study	——	——
opportunities for promotion	——	——

Subsidised meals

Spacious, airy working conditions

It may be interesting to look at the choices of others in your group and discuss how different they are. You could make a block graph (histogram) of them.

1.5 How much do you know about jobs?

Exercise 6

Look at the exercise on the opposite page. You can do it either on your own or in a group, for here several heads may be better than one. Consider either three jobs of your own choosing, or three jobs suggested by your tutor, and deal with them in the following way. Copy out the table using a different symbol for each job, perhaps ✓, 0 and Ø; and, considering one job at a time, write its symbol in what you believe to be the correct column opposite each statement. Repeat this procedure for the next job, and finally for the third. You may be surprised to see how many features different jobs have in common.

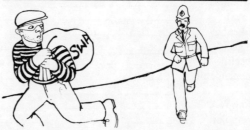

1.6 Personal qualities at work

But what about the need for personal qualities in different jobs? For example, it might not be very wise to entrust the job of handling money to a person who was inclined to gamble! You may have read,

Conditions	always	sometimes	occasionally	never
long periods away from home				
regular eight-hour days				
foreman or supervisor always present				
a night-shift				
looking after trainees				
several jobs included in work-load				
outdoor work mainly				
working as part of a team				

Requirements	always	sometimes	occasionally	never
being able to stand for long periods				
physical fitness				
keen attention				
uniform				
special clothing				
being able to express facts clearly in writing				
being able to learn to use mechanical objects quickly				
smart appearance				
a first-aid certificate				
being able to speak a language other than English				
a minimum height				
willingness to take risks				

earlier in this book, how important it is to match your job to your personality. You can see in the next exercise that this may not be as easy as it sounds.

Exercise 7

The importance of character, personality and health when choosing a job

On the next page is a table showing some occupations. Beneath it are numbered columns of qualities you need to be successful in various jobs. Copy out the table and, in the space beneath each job, write the *numbers* of the qualities you think a person needs in order to be able to do that job well. For example, if you feel that for a particular job you need tact, kindness and strength, write 1, 4, and 10 in the space for the job. This exercise can be quite difficult and will need careful thought, so take your time.

Nurse	Postman/lady
Bank cashier	Sales assistant
Car assembly worker	Van driver
Police officer	Cook
Teacher	Garage mechanic
Hairdresser	Caretaker

Qualities
1 *tact*
2 *sympathy*
3 *firmness*
4 *kindness*
5 *carefulness*

6 *quickness*
7 *liking people*
8 *smart appearance*
9 *liking children*
10 *strength*
11 *strong hands*
12 *good health*
13 *being active*
14 *being well-spoken*
15 *being good-looking*
16 *height*
17 *being easy-going*
18 *confidence*
19 *a sense of humour*
20 *friendliness*
21 *efficiency*
22 *honesty*
23 *reliability*
24 *trustworthiness*
25 *punctuality*
26 *neat writing*
27 *tolerance*
28 *ability to work without supervision*
29 *ability to get on with all ages*
30 *willingness to work long hours*
31 *not being easily bored*
32 *ability to use own initiative*
33 *resourcefulness*
34 *carefulness about cleanliness*
35 *fondness for hard work*
36 *patience*
37 *ability to work in a team*
38 *preparedness for a long period of training*

1.7 Job planning

In everyday life, at home, on holiday, at work, you have to meet and try to get on with many other people. Some may tend to rub you up the wrong way, while others will make you feel pleased to be with them. How good are you at relating to others even when they are difficult to get on with?

Do the next exercise honestly and see what picture of yourself appears. Copy out the form and complete it, choosing your own words or comments to answer the questions.

What personal qualities are needed in these jobs?

Exercise 8

How good are you at coping with:

being bored?	_____
being made angry?	_____
being unfairly treated?	_____
being tired?	_____
being under pressure?	_____
working unsupervised?	_____
working in poor conditions?	_____
being bossed about?	_____
a rapidly changing situation?	_____
making decisions?	_____
working in a team?	_____
organising people?	_____
keeping people happy?	_____
taking responsibility?	_____
smoothing over quarrels?	_____
being firm with people?	_____
getting people to work together?	_____
understanding people?	_____
sympathising with people?	_____
being patient with people?	_____

(cont.)

You and the future

Would you like to work
mostly outdoors or mostly
indoors? _____

with other people or on your
own? _____

in one place or travelling
about? _____

near home or away from
home? _____

Are you prepared to spend
several years training for a
job? _____

Are you prepared to give up
free time to help your job (for
example by attending evening
classes)? _____

Do you care more about
whether the job is interesting
than about how much you
would earn? _____

Do you have a job in mind
already? If so, what? _____

Why do you want this to be
your job? _____

What work would your parents
like you to do? _____

Are they pushing you in this
direction? _____

If so, is this OK by you or
against your will? _____

Are you prepared to stay on at
school and get all the
qualifications which the school
recommends? _____

Would your parents let you
stay on? _____

Would they have financial
problems if you did? _____

Add anything else you like
about your strengths,
personality and hopes. _____

1.8 What do you value?

Values are the principles, likes and
ambitions which are important to you *now;*
you may admire, enjoy doing or very much
want these things in your life – for
example, living at home, playing games,

obtaining O-levels, being popular, going to
parties. Not all values need be serious
ambitions; they can just as easily relate to
your spare-time activities – and, of course,
values change with time. You are not likely
to have the same values now as five years
ago, or five years ahead. Certainly you will
not have quite the same values as others,
though you may have values in common
with them.

Exercise 9

Copy out the table below and complete it,
following the instructions on page 13.

column 1	col. 2	col. 3	col. 4	col. 5	col. 6	col. 7	col. 8
1							
2							
3							
4							
5							
6							
7							
8							
9							
10							
11							
12							
13							
14							
15							
16							

col. 1 Name sixteen things you value; for example, being honest, getting four O-levels, having a pet, etc.

col. 2 Tick those which you feel would be of use in your career, or which you would like to do as a job.

col. 3 Tick those which involve helping others in some way.

col. 4 Tick those which involve manual skills of any kind.

col. 5 Tick those which you would have included in your list two years ago.

col. 6 Tick those which require physical fitness, either for indoor or outdoor activities.

col. 7 Tick those which involve thought or study.

col. 8 Tick those which your parents would include in their own list of values.

You might also like to extend this table to show
a) how expensive these values are. What does each cost per month?
b) which do you do alone and which in the company of others?
Have a good careful look at your answers and in a few sentences say what the table tells you about yourself.

To analyse your personal values further, try the 'game of fives':

Exercise 10

a) Which five of your achievements or attitudes are you most pleased about?
b) If you only had five years to live, what five things would you most like to do or achieve?
c) Who are the five most important people in your life – those who have influenced you most?
d) If you could keep only five of all your present possessions what would they be?

Now look carefully at your answers and see how they compare with what you have said about yourself in the previous exercise. What conclusions can you draw about yourself? What do these two exercises tell you about your character and personality? Has anything you have discovered about yourself surprised you?

1.9 Some questions

What help has this unit been?

1 How far has this unit helped you to understand yourself better? Very much? Quite a lot? A little? Not at all? Comments, please!
2 What new things do you know about yourself?
3 What new hopes have you discovered?
4 What has seemed to you to be the most important discovery you have made about yourself from this work?
5 In what ways do you feel able to help a particular relative or fellow-student to understand him- or herself better?
6 Please make written suggestions of anything that could be added to this unit, and discuss them with your tutor. Ask your tutor to send them to the author – or, better still, write to him yourself, at the publisher's address. Your ideas may well be included if this book is revised in future.
7 Following from what you have discovered about yourself,
a) what action will you take to put right your weak points?
b) how do you plan to strengthen your strong points?

Unit 2 The choice is yours

Some decisions are taken by others, and you have to abide by them. For example, whether to join the Common Market, whether you can vote at a certain age, whether you have to go to prison and whether you have to attend school. Think of ten more.

Some decisions are usually made on your own. For example, who you sit by in class, how you spend your pocket-money, what you do at break, whether you smoke and who your best friend shall be. Think of ten more.

Some decisions are usually made by you, but after talking to others. For example, how long you spend on homework, what your hairstyle should be, whether to try to become a youth-club secretary and what job you should take up as a career. Think of ten more.

But, whether you like it or not, all your decisions are influenced by what other people think. For example, do you choose clothes to please yourself, or to impress other people such as your friends? Whom do you try to please most?

Where do you get your ideas about yourself from? If you regard yourself as quick-tempered, or honest, it is usually only because someone else has already told you that you are like that! Suppose your father or mother says you are quick-tempered, and your girlfriend or boyfriend says you are not, whom do you believe?

It is natural that you should value some people's opinions and comments more than others – but who is right? Is anyone right? In fact, is it possible simply to be yourself, to decide for yourself, at all? Anyone who succeeds in being himself or herself is often the subject of criticism, or praise, from many directions.

2.1 Taking decisions

Everyone takes many decisions every day. But some are made without much thought – in fact, they may not seem to be decisions at all. They are habits. Make a list of your own habits or routines before you go to sleep. In what order do you do the following: take off your clothes, wash, clean your teeth, arrange your things for morning, etc.?

Yet these habits do represent decisions. Although there might be a row if, for example, you did not get up, it could be quite difficult for someone to make you get up if you had firmly decided against it. On the other hand, the consequences – angry parents, angry teachers, an empty stomach – might mean it was not worth your while. But, once up, must you wash? *Ought* you to wash?

How often do you make such automatic decisions, not thinking about the alternatives and their consequences?

Other decisions may be given a little thought, but still not seem like major ones. Which present to buy? How to spend the weekend? There are yet others, however, which affect your life very much, and therefore need considerable thought. These are the ones you will often not be able to make without help and advice. For example, whether to drop a school subject, whether to marry and whether to live away from home.

Checkmate I think.....

Not the way I play!

14

In many cases there will be several *alternative solutions* to the problem; and different solutions may suit different people, so that there is often no single 'correct' answer. You may be the sort of person who will take a high risk if you stand to gain a lot; on the other hand, you may not want the chance of losing at all.

So, when making important decisions, you should ask:
a) what are the alternatives?
b) which suits me best?
c) is the risk worth the possible gain?
d) can I make the decision on my own, or do I need advice and information from others to help me make up my mind?
e) will the decision affect me alone, or others as well?

Exercise 1

Charles Mumford, awakened by his wife hitting him with the morning paper, sat up, rubbed his eyes and thought about the day ahead. Need he shave until the evening? He thought he really should. What about two slices of toast? His bathroom scales hinted that a second was not necessary, but Charles liked that particular brand of marmalade. . . .

Then he thought about the morning's work. A science test for 2A? Or should he let them do the second half of the topic and test them on all of it? He was not fond of marking - but perhaps the little horrors could mark each other's under his direction. Better not, though: they could cheat, or simply mark wrongly, and at the end of the year that might make all the difference as to whether they joined a more able or less able group, and might therefore even affect their later opportunities.

His mind wandered on. He did not like his nickname, 'Mummy', but should he grumble if he heard that aggressive fourth-year lout use it, or would it be better to laugh it off by saying, perhaps, that he had not yet had the necessary operation? Then there was the problem of staff absence. Ought he to indicate that he might not be able to sit with a history class, because he

should really see the training manager of the nearby engineering firm, or would it be more considerate to help out?

What he really must do this week, however, was to make up his mind whether to apply for the head-of-department job at Grange School, about twenty-five miles away. Suppose he got the job, ought he to move house? Did he want to? Did his wife want to? Should he really apply for the job at all? If there were a large number of applicants, what chance did he stand of getting it anyway? Perhaps he would have that second slice of toast - and an extra cup of tea, too!

Now there was the evening's marking and lesson preparation to consider. He wondered whether there would be time to see his sister-in-law in hospital, or whether he should wait until he had rather less to do. He might not be able to go if he agreed to referee that football match straight after school. And what about the talk to the Wine Circle tomorrow evening? How many sample bottles ought he to take? Could he really spare any of his rare and good elderflower wine, now eight years old?

When he finally left for school, he kissed his patient and long-suffering wife on the cheek and discovered, five minutes later, that his car battery was flat. Damn, he thought. Bus, bike or taxi?

a) How many decisions can you find in the passage?
b) Which of them would he probably have made automatically, with little or no thought?
c) Which might he have thought about but not considered a major decision?
d) Which were the major decisions facing him?
e) Does the passage tell you anything about Charles Mumford's personality?
f) What decisions have you had to make today? List as many as you can.
g) Which of these do you regard as having been the most important? Explain why.

Which is the best alternative?

2.2 Alternative solutions

Exercise 2

Working either on your own or in groups, arrive at a decision or plan of action for each of the problems described below.

Remember that

a) more than one solution is possible in most cases, and you must decide

    i) which is the best for you, according to your opinions and values;

    ii) what alternatives, however unlikely, you are rejecting.

b) if possible, you should try to recognise *why* you make the choice you do.

Set A

i) Some simple situations. Write your decisions in the form of a table, stating the problem in the first column, your answer in the second and the alternative(s) you reject in the third. It may help to cast your mind back to your first day in school, or to imagine that you are a pupil in another school, or have just started work.

    a) You get lost when sent with a message.

    b) You do not know where to go for your next session.

    c) You lose your anorak.

    d) You feel sick.

    e) You lose your meal voucher.

    f) You arrive late.

    g) You are bullied by an older student or employee.

    h) Your PE kit or tool-box is stolen.

    i) Your parents want to visit your tutor or supervisor to discuss your work.

    j) You miss the last bus home.

    k) You have to go to the dentist in school- or work-time.

ii) Some slightly more difficult situations. Deal with them in the same way as the last lot.

    a) Your friend asks you to steal a kitchen knife.

    b) Your parents have asked you to baby-sit but you want to go to a disco.

    c) You are travelling on the bus with a sixteen-year-old friend. Do you say you are under fourteen to get a reduced fare?

    d) You tell your parents you will be in by 10.30 p.m. You are invited to a party while you are out, and you know that if you go you will be very late.

    e) You have been accused of damaging some furniture. You did not do it but you know who did. Should you say who the culprit is? Give reasons for your decision.

iii) You have saved all but £500 towards your first new car. For the money you have, you see an advertisement for a two-year-old secondhand one of the same make, with extras such as a radio. The car is said to be in good condition. Would you change your plan? What enquiries would you make before buying the secondhand car?

iv) You look older than you are. Your friends urge you to go to a pub although you are still under age.

v) You work in a shop. A friend's brother comes in. When he goes, you see a penknife is missing. There are no other customers.

vi) What could you do about a local leisure spot which has become so polluted that it is no longer fit for swimming, fishing or camping, or even to walk about in? It might help to imagine that you feel angry about it.

vii) Your bedroom needs decorating. Your parents keep nagging you about it. They feel you ought to do it, and have already decided not to do it themselves, but would buy the materials you would need to do the job. It is summer and the longer evenings would enable you to do it in daylight, but you like to go swimming most evenings. A friend could help you - but may then ask you to help dig up some potatoes in his own parents' allotment. You do not swim often in winter, but you also know it is better to decorate a room in daylight.

Set B

i) Nick is a popular and capable twenty-eight-year-old who can turn his hand to anything. He works for a large branch of a national hardware firm, having sold his own glazing business two years ago. He is ambitious and hopes his wife will agree to his doing similar work in an Arab country as a senior manager. He can go out there for four months to look at the opportunities and help start up the business. His wife and young daughter will not be able to go with him immediately. Later, however, if business is good, he could rent a bungalow there and bring them out. (His wife's parents live about ten miles from where Nick and his family live at present.)

After the four months Nick might be able to come home; but on the other hand the firm might require him to stay on to build up the business, which would mean that his wife would have all the problems of selling the house, letting it furnished or deciding not to go. If she decided to go they would return after four years, or could have an annual holiday of eight weeks and remain abroad for ten years.

What problems could arise
a) for Nick?
b) for his wife?
c) concerning his two-year-old daughter?

Imagine you are Nick or his wife.
ii) Find out why you live at your present address. What factors would make you want to move?

iii) The Browns want to decide who uses the family car on Friday nights.

Mrs Brown wants a lift to and from the supermarket with the weekend shopping. She wants to get there about seven p.m. and leave at eight p.m., when it closes. She does not like shopping in very crowded shops on Saturdays. Mr Brown, who is the only driver in the family, uses the car for work during the week and gets home at 6.30 p.m. on Fridays. If Mrs Brown arrives much after seven p.m., many of the goods she wants are sold out.

Since they first bought the car a year ago, Mr Brown has given his son Bill a lift to the swimming club on Friday evenings. Bill has to be there at about seven. He needs a lift if he is to have time to come home, have a snack and still get to the baths on time. However, he is quite happy to make his own way home at the end of the evening.

Mr Brown is a keen domino player, and likes to get two hours in at the local pub on Friday nights. The pub is a couple of miles from home in the opposite direction to Bill's club, so Mr Brown usually drops Bill, then drives on to his pub and practises until about 9.15 p.m.

Christine, his daughter, is not interested in using the family car. On Fridays she goes out with her boyfriend Andrew, who picks her up in his sports car and drives her to a disco, often passing Bill's swimming baths.
iv) A family of four have a very old television set that keeps breaking down. It is not working at all at the moment. They are all wondering whether it is really worth getting it repaired, because that would cost not less than £16. Perhaps they would be better off getting a new set on HP, or hiring one. Dad does not want to spend any more money on repairs, now or later. On the other hand he wants to lay out only the smallest initial payment if they decide to buy on HP or to hire.

The daughter definitely thinks that they ought to get another set. She thinks their present one is old-fashioned. Also she would like a portable one to take up to her bedroom late at night. The son would like to watch some programmes on BBC-2, and their present set does not receive this channel. Moreover, he thinks the picture is poor. Mother thinks the old set is all right, though she would not object to a new one. But she does not want the family to get into debt.

A new black and white set for cash costs £60 for a portable, and £120 for a 23" table model; to buy on HP requires an initial payment of £20, and £5 per month for two years. Renting or hiring a set costs £6 per month. Colour sets cost twice as much as black and white ones.

v) In answering this question you have to put yourself in the positions of several different people. It is important to think out how different decisions will affect those people in different ways.

a) A mother of two children, aged ten and five, is trying to decide whether to go back to the same kind of job she did before she had her family. Her husband is not at all keen on the idea of his wife's going out to work, but they find it difficult to make ends meet. The youngest child has just started school.

b) A young woman in her mid-twenties is trying to decide whether to take up the tempting offer of a job with an engineering company in Canada. She has a fiancé whose job will keep him in this country. She also has rather elderly parents who are not at all well. The only other member of the family, her twenty-two-year-old brother, takes very little interest in his parents' welfare.

c) A young man of twenty-two is engaged to a girl he has known since they were both children. His parents are good friends of her parents. The couple have been planning to get married during the next two years. The young man is sent away from home by the firm he works for, and meets another girl he likes very much. This girl is from a richer family than his and when he brings her home it is obvious his parents do not like her.

d) A man of fifty-five is trying to decide whether to give up teaching ten years before the age at which he would have

to retire. Although he is deputy head of his school, he is rather bored with the routine of his job. He has always been a very keen gardener and thinks he should be able to buy enough land somewhere in the south-west of England to set up a small market garden. His family have grown up and left home, but his wife does not like the idea of leaving her family and friends in the northern industrial town where they live at present.

2.3 Strategies

When you reach the end of the fifth year at school, at least ten alternatives may be open to you:

a) staying at school for a one-year sixth-form course;

b) staying at school for a two-year A-level course;

c) a full-time general course at a college of further education;

d) a full-time vocational course at a college of further education;

e) work, with education on a sandwich or block-release basis;

f) work, with day-release;

g) work full-time, with no other education;

h) apprenticeship training, with the whole of your first year at college fully paid for by your employer;

i) an inevitable period of unemployment, but an opportunity to join several possible work-preparation or work-experience schemes to enable you to become more skilled (your local careers office will supply all the information about such schemes - see exercise 8 below);

j) lazing around on the dole;

k) getting married and hoping to survive on social security payments.

Most young people endeavour to fall into groups a) to h). Therefore they may wish to consider *strategies*. A strategy is a plan of action. There are:

a) *safe strategies:* plans which offer least risk and most probable result;

b) *escape strategies:* plans which avoid the worst possible result;

c) *wish strategies:* aiming for what you really want and ignoring all risk of failure;
d) *best-hope strategies:* a combination of any of the three above.

Exercise 3

Sam is in his fifth year at school, taking several GCEs and CSEs, and is wondering what to do next year. He wants to be a mechanical engineer in the aircraft industry. Several options are open to him:
a) he could easily be accepted as a garage mechanic and study engineering at his local college of further education;
b) he could possibly take the appropriate A-levels, and then a degree if he were clever enough, but he is not sure about this;
c) he could do a full-time course at a polytechnic;
d) he could apply for a technician apprenticeship at a large firm of aero-engineers and follow their training programme, with college day- or block-release.

Each of the following decisions represents a possible *strategy* Sam could adopt. Which decision fits each strategy?
a) He will take up a garage mechanic's job (and certainly be a good mechanic when trained).

Technician training can take place in college, at a training centre and on-the-job

What may have influenced this young woman's decision in her choice of job?

jobs, but now finds it difficult, because of his past, to get further employment. His mates offer him very little advice, although he really would like to train for any one of a variety of jobs.

b) After five years of study, Sally is a good pianist. She also likes hotel and bar work, waitressing and serving drinks. She would like to teach music, but while working on holiday at a hotel on the south coast she is invited to join a small local orchestra. What is more, the hotel are so pleased with her dining-room and bar work that they offer her permanent employment. She loves being with young children.

c) Peter Arrowsmith is a lecturer in English at a university, earning a good salary. He enjoys writing stories and plays. He is offered an extra £2,000 a year to become an editor for a publishing firm, where he would be kept very much busier. He has a family of four, two of whom are still at secondary school and one in junior school; Steven, the eldest, is about to start a university course himself.

Exercise 5

Divorce?

Brian is an office worker. He earns £50 per week, and is thirty years old. He likes gardening and doing odd jobs around the house. The mortgage and family expenses make overtime necessary three nights a week. He married Christine, who was an office worker, too, before marriage. She is now at home with two children under school age. She is bored with housework, but she is a keen amateur dancer, and has reached quite a high standard with her partner, who is not married and earns £80 per week. Brian and Christine have been married for five years and for the past twelve months have quarrelled frequently.

a) Write down some of the arguments each might use against the other.

b) What advice would you give to i) Brian, and ii) Christine?

c) Do you think it would be better for them to part or see it through?
Remember they have two small children. Give reasons for your opinion.

b) So as not to fail a course, Sam will not enrol on one, except at the lowest level necessary.

c) He will do A-levels, and hope to join the firm as an undergraduate apprentice, studying for his degree at a university or polytechnic.

d) He will become a technician apprentice and hope to achieve much the same as in c) - but this way it may take a little longer.

Exercise 4

Now you have had some practice in the art of decision-making, say what are the options, for the following people, and which you would recommend. Work as individuals or in small groups.

a) Norman was expelled from school for stealing just under a month before he was due to leave. He has tried a number of odd

Exercise 6

Bearing in mind what you now know about decision-making and about how you decide, which of the following points would you consider if you were faced with the following problems? (You would not need to consider all the points each time.) Make a grid or chart showing your answers.

Problems

a) buying a birthday present;
b) buying yourself some shoes;
c) deciding to drop a school subject;
d) deciding whether to accept an invitation;
e) deciding whether to join a sports club;
f) deciding whether to marry;
g) deciding which job to aim for.

Considerations

a) How readily available are the things you require?
b) How much information do you have or would you need?
c) Would you allow yourself to be persuaded or insist on choosing for yourself?
d) How important would pleasure, satisfaction and sense of achievement be in your decision?
e) Would you choose something you *needed*, or something you would just like to have (either for yourself or others)?
f) Would your choice suit your personality – and should it?
g) Whose advice, if any, would you ask for or require?
h) Would your choice match your skills or abilities – and should it?

2.4 Obtaining help

Exercise 7

In the last exercise, and in earlier work, you read of 'advice' – but whose advice? Consider whom you could consult when choosing a job:
a) your parents or relatives;
b) your friends;
c) your head teacher;
d) your subject teacher;
e) your form/class tutor or teacher;
f) your careers teacher;
g) college of further education staff;
h) your careers officer;
i) local employers;
j) employers' publications.
Each can help you in different ways. Produce a list of what help you could obtain from each of these sources, and say when their help might be limited or non-existent. When you have done this, discuss your findings with your teacher and other members of your class.

Exercise 8

You should also obtain the following information and make a note of it:
Who is your careers officer?
Where is your careers office?
When is your careers officer in school?
How can you or your parents get in touch with your careers officer at other times?
What is the variety of help your careers officer or careers office can provide?

Maybe your school careers library is organised according to the Careers Library Classification Index system. If so, it is useful to know the system's main groupings of careers:
A   college, polytechnic and university prospectuses;
B   the armed forces;
C   management, administration, central and local government, the civil service;
D   unclassified;
E   fine arts, design, graphic art, fashion and textile design;
F   teaching, library work, languages, cultural occupations, religion;
G   music, drama, sport, dance, radio and TV work, entertainment, recreation;
H   publishing, printing, journalism;
I   hotel work, catering, home economics, laundry work, dry cleaning, hairdressing, beauty culture;
J   health and hospital jobs, the health service, all types of nursing, dentistry, optician and allied professions, midwifery, medical laboratory technician, radiography, physiotherapy, osteotherapy, speech therapy, dietetics;

K   all kinds of social and community welfare work, the probation service;
L   the law: solicitor, barrister, legal executive;
M   security and protection, the police, customs and excise, the prison service;
N   all kinds of finance: insurance, bank work, accountancy, building societies;
O   all kinds of marketing, buying, selling; the distributive trades, advertising;
P   management, economics, work with computers, work study (see also C);
Q   the sciences (see also J);
R   all kinds of engineering: auto-, aero-, agricultural, chemical, electrical, gas, heat, light, mechanical, mining, production;
S   manufacturing and processing technology;
T   manufacturing and processing at craft level;
U   building, civil engineering, land services, surveying, etc.;
V   unclassified;
W   agriculture, horticulture, work with animals;
X   transport and materials handling by road, rail and sea; the merchant navy, the fishing fleet, inland waterways;
Y   unclassified;
Z   opportunities overseas.

The best way for you to use this list is to read it through carefully and put a circle round the initial letters of all job-areas in which you are interested. You can then easily find material which may interest you. A school cannot guarantee to have information about every job but, if you wish to know more about a job, they can either ring the careers office for you, send to a firm or organisation for information, or at least give you an address to which you can write for details. In the last case it is a good idea to discuss your letter with your English or careers teacher, and show him or her the final copy before you send it.

Many careers centres remain open later than usual on one evening each week. Why not visit your centre and ask for the information you require?

The illustration given below shows the kind of information an employer would give to the careers office when notifying them of a vacancy. Look at it carefully. Can you think of any other useful information the employer might provide?

General Vacancy Card

Classification	Employer	Tel No......	Nature of work offered
	Name		
Industry	Address		
	....		
Occupation	Trade or business		Qualification/experience required
Interview arrangements		Wages	
		16 17	
		18½ 17½	

	Hours		*Further Education and Training*	Age	Prospects
Start Finish	Total weekly	Day Release			
5/5½ days		Course			
Lunch ½ day					

2.5 Choosing for exams

During the third year of secondary education you will probably be asked to make choices of subjects to study in the fourth and fifth years. These will be finalised in the summer term. The choices you make will be the result of discussion between yourself, your parents and your teachers. There will be plenty of time for them, provided you take the opportunity of finding out all you can about any jobs you have in mind.

In most cases your choices will lead to your being entered for those subjects in public examinations. These are

a) The General Certificate of Education (GCE)

The usual age for sitting GCE O-level is sixteen, but you can enter earlier or later; you can even take O-levels when you have left school. Most of these examinations occur during June. You can be entered for as many subjects as you are capable of tackling;

b) The Certificate of Secondary Education (CSE)

You have to be sixteen or nearly sixteen, and still full-time at school, to take CSE exams. They are taken at about the same time as GCEs and in the same set of circumstances. Again, you can be entered for as many subjects as you are capable of studying.

The following is an approximate indication of the meaning the grades have:

GCE

A extremely able in the subject;
B good: above average for the range of ability for which the examination is intended;
C average in the subject for this ability range;
D only fair: most employers and colleges do not regard this grade as a pass, but more like a CSE grade 2;
E rather weak: you will either have found the subject very difficult, or not have worked as you should;
U unclassified: did you take the correct decision when you chose this subject?

CSE

1 very good for the ability range for which the examination is intended: this grade is regarded by most, if not all, employers and colleges as being equivalent to a GCE pass;
2 a good, above-average pass;
3 an average-standard pass;
4 a pass slightly below average ability;
5 rather poor.

It is interesting to note that the average ability of *all* young people is about CSE grade 3. However, *the important thing is that you do your best*, so that you have the satisfaction of achieving as good a result as you can.

If a subject is offered at 'Sixteen-Plus' level and you do not gain an O-level pass, you will be given the appropriate CSE pass. However, not many subjects are available at Sixteen-Plus as yet.

If you study a subject at 'Mode 1' you will be following the syllabus set by the examination board, and your examination papers will be sent away to be marked. A Mode 3 course, however, follows a syllabus designed by your teachers, who will also have decided how best to award a final grade. Usually a proportion of the marks can be earned in several important tests or an examination, and the rest by your own projects, research and classwork. No two Mode 3 courses are exactly alike, though very careful precautions are taken regarding the standards needed to obtain various grades.

Which subjects shall I choose?

First of all, *what about a job?*
Young people have
a) no idea about a job yet;
b) a romantic or fantasy idea, not based on their ability;
c) a vague idea; or
d) definite hopes and plans.
- but most people aged thirteen or fourteen are in the first category!

Two important points to note are
a) most people are quite capable of doing any one of several jobs equally well;
b) in this day and age, it may well be that

your first job will not turn out to be your only one, because jobs can cease to exist, and new ones be created.

So choose a broadly based course to give you a good general education – and do not reject a subject just because you do not get on with the tutor. Doing so may close the door on the very job you want.

Before you even start to make the choice, you will be given the opportunity to find out a great deal about any ideas you have at the moment. Colleges, universities, and employers look for people with an all-round education as well as for people with special aptitudes.

To help you obtain this broad background certain subjects may be compulsory, at levels suited to your ability.

English

This is the most important ingredient of all in your education. It enables you to express yourself in your own language with accuracy and fluency, and it forms a basis for all your other subjects.

Maths

Another very important foundation subject. *Very few* jobs indeed require no maths, which is usually a compulsory subject and always an important one in combination with others.

What are you going to be when you grow up?

A language

You are not the only person in the world, nor are we the only nation. Being able to speak and write another language is of especial importance now that we are Europeans.

Science

Very important in understanding the modern world. All sciences are of equal academic value, but physics is probably the most useful in terms of jobs. You may want to do more than one science. Chemistry and physics are a good combination – the cornerstones of most careers in science – and so are chemistry and biology. A third good combination is biology, chemistry and geography. Even if you have no idea of pursuing a scientific career, you may well find that science provides useful background knowledge for many jobs, such as secretarial work, marketing, and sales and personnel work.

Technical drawing

Combined with physics, this is a very important subject if you intend to follow a career in engineering or construction at any level. It can also be useful coupled with a craft such as woodwork or metalwork.

Humanities

These include history, geography, religious education and music. Each of these is a useful academic subject to have, and may well be required as a qualification for a large number of jobs, especially those involving helping people.

Commercial subjects

Shorthand, typing, business studies. A good introduction to careers in this area. Typing can be a useful skill, but do not neglect other subjects. Many firms prefer a good background, and make provision for you to learn clerical skills when you join them, at a 'tech'.

It is important that you should enjoy your fourth and fifth years. But some people have to choose between a subject they like and a more useful one, so think very carefully of your future before choosing finally. If you already know what you want your career to be, you can choose with that in mind. Many careers have specific entry requirements. However, many people make their career decisions over a period of time. You may well have a broad area of interest in mind, such as 'helping people', 'making things' or 'doing something scientific'. If this is the case, find out all you can about jobs in the area concerned.

Useful sources in any careers library are
a) *The Careers Guide*, published by HMSO;
b) the 'Choice of Career' booklets by HMSO;
c) 'If I Were A' career leaflets – there are eighty of these: each is a simple leaflet, outlining the skills and kinds of work in various careers, and there will probably be a copy of the title list on your noticeboard;
d) *Careers* by Ruth Miller: costing about £1.50 from Penguin Books, this is a useful guide to many careers;
e) the Signposts system (see p. 40);
f) *Your Choice at 13-Plus* – a *very* useful book, published by CRAC (Careers Research and Advisory Centre);
g) the 'Close Up' series published by COIC (Careers and Occupational Information Centre).
Keep your own record of your investigations.

2.6 Some questions

How much use has this unit been to you?
1 a) How would you choose a friend of the opposite sex? To suit you, even if your partner were disapproved of by your friends? Or would you choose someone whom your friends would like, or even be envious about? Would you only choose a friend of whom your parents would approve, or would you oppose or even be prepared to shock your parents?
b) Do you know of people who have married their boss's son or daughter? Do you think they married for love or for convenience? Why do you think this?
2 Has this unit helped you to understand more clearly how you make personal decisions? Comments, please.
3 Identify those decisions in the unit which were related to you
a) as an individual;
b) as a young worker;
c) as a member of a community.
4 Do you think that people should make decisions with as little regard as possible to the wishes and opinions of others? Or is it sometimes wiser to take the views of other people into account? Try to find examples. (Sometimes magazines have personal or 'agony' columns, which discuss problems of this kind. Find some and discuss them with your group.) What alternative solutions would you offer to some of the personal problems you have met or know about among your friends?

Unit 3 Thinking about work

Within a year or two you will be leaving school - or you may even have recently left - to continue your education and training on a full-time basis in a college of further education, in a university or elsewhere; to look for a job; or to find some other way of making an adult contribution to the community. Adult life can offer opportunities to obtain great pleasure outside the paid job you chose or may find it necessary to do. Look for examples of adults who find such satisfaction - for example, Red Cross work, hang-gliding, growing prize vegetables. No doubt you know many more illustrations. Compare your ideas and examples with those of your friends.

But often adults give their whole lives and attention to their work, and have few or no interests outside it. Can you provide some examples of this from your own experience? Perhaps you will be able to discuss these with your tutor.

Either way, it is accepted that all adults will do work of some kind in order to have a recognised place in their community - although such work need not always be *paid*.

During the course of this unit it is hoped that you will have work experience, visits to firms or talks from employers, so that you can get a chance to develop realistic ideas about working life.

3.1 Why work?

People go to work for several reasons; earning money is only one of them. Many people get pleasure from doing their jobs or seeing the product of their work. Many find it important to be in the company of others, and many who need to live a full and interesting life find work helps them to do so.

But, of course, if you look at the economics of work you see it is a cycle of events.

Exercise 1

That is really a very simple illustration, because our earnings pay for many services as well as goods, and because some of our earnings are often saved. But you can see that, if the circle is broken at any point, the result must be that many people will lose their jobs. If the speed of events slows down, money circulates more slowly and trade becomes worse; this will lead to what is known as a 'slump'. If trade picks up and there is a much bigger demand for goods, and if the manufacturers can supply them on time, that is called a 'boom'. Now choose a point at which the circle might be broken, and illustrate the situation with a diagram of your own.

Exercise 2

Industry and employment fall into the following major categories; for each one give three more examples.

a) *Obtaining raw materials:* for example, prospecting for and obtaining oil.

b) *Processing these raw materials:* for example, making engines, motor tyres, sulphuric acid, cosmetics, etc.

c) *Distributing all kinds of materials, goods, people, etc.:* for example, via oil-tankers, GPO vans, supermarkets and British Rail.

d) *Servicing industries and agencies:* these provide services of all kinds, from governments to cinemas – that is, they meet needs and wishes at various levels. Financial needs are met by banks (among others), and legal needs by solicitors. Other examples:

Administrative needs are met by regional health authorities (and what else?)

Community needs are met by social services departments (and what else?)

Entertainment needs are met by bingo halls and theatres (and what else?)

A cadet on board an oil tanker

Examples of the finished product

27

3.2 Training in industry and commerce

Business and industry need properly trained, skilled employees at all levels to carry out this work. But people have almost always learned their jobs by watching somebody experienced and copying his or her methods. In more recent years, a few firms have provided methodical training, but these have mainly been the larger ones, and many workers have not benefited from it.

There are many clear disadvantages to this situation:
a) the quality of training for a given job varies tremendously from firm to firm;
b) training standards and methods vary widely because of the lack of any advisory body;
c) experienced workers may or may not be good at their jobs, and in any case are not trained in the art of teaching others;
d) because training is not organised it occupies too little or, more frequently, too much time;
e) young people spend too much time on menial tasks rather than learning the skills of the job;
f) some categories of staff, such as clerical workers, receive virtually no organised training;
g) there is little off-the-job training in special workshops because of the cost of equipping and running such centres.
The haphazard approach to training has two main results:
a) firms which give training are subsidising firms which do not, by providing them with trained staff;
b) in many occupations there is a persistent shortage of trained manpower, which limits industry's capacity to expand.

The main problems confronting industry have been to ensure that
a) there is an adequate supply of trained workers
b) that the quality of training is continually improved, and
c) that the cost of training is fairly distributed.

From 1964 to 1981 this was generally undertaken by the Industrial Training Boards (ITBs) of which there were about 24, advising the bulk of manufacturing industry. However in the autumn of 1981 the government decided that it would set up alternative controls of training and education for young people, and at the same time invite many industries to prepare and operate their own training programmes as they felt best according to the needs of the particular industries. Only six of the original training boards remain. They are:

Construction ITB
Radnor House
1272 London Road
Norbury
London SW16 4EL

Engineering Careers Information Service
54 Clarendon Road
Watford
Herts WD1 1LB

Hotel and Catering IRB
Ramsey House
Central Square
Wembley
Middlesex HA9 7AP

Clothing and Allied Products ITB
10th Floor
Tower House
Merrion Way
Leeds LS2 8NY

Road Transport ITB
Capitol House
Empire Way
Wembley
Middlesex HA9 ONG

Rubber and Plastics Processing ITB
Brent House
950 Great West Road
Brentford
Middlesex TW8 9ES

Many industries have a wider range of jobs within them than many people realise; take for example the Distribution Industry.

One of the characteristics of distribution is the wide range of jobs available. These include:

sales assistants: probably the largest group numerically – responsible for dealing with customers, pricing, clearing and often displaying stock, and dealing with cash and paperwork;

sales representatives: selling direct from wholesalers to the customer, and doing administration;

telephone sales staff: in wholesale companies, taking orders by telephone;

clerical staff: responsible for working with cash, customers' orders and invoices, and for general administration – found particularly in head offices, mail-order companies and large wholesalers;

computer work: many wholesalers, large retailers and mail-order companies use sophisticated computer systems;

display staff: responsible for designing and producing window and internal display – may work alone or in a team;

managers: a very large group, ranging from store managers to those managing a small department; whose three main areas of responsibility are staff, customers and stock, with administration often a major concern as well;

buyers: those who select and negotiate for the merchandise to be stocked by a company – frequently work in teams in a head office, but many department stores have a buyer for each department;

general management: promotion leads to area management, supervising a number of outlets, or to one of a large variety of head-office management and administration posts;

merchandising: involves responsibility for the design and layout of stores or warehouses;

personnel and training: at head office or branch levels, many people move into this area from within the industry;

warehousemen: responsible for checking, handling and storing stock and doing associated paperwork;

transport management: responsible for organising the movement of goods and/or vehicles, and the delivery of orders.

The following tables show levels of achievement needed at school, details of training and examples of the types of job available in

a) distribution; b) engineering;
c) motor manufacture.

For years there has been an attitude maintained by employers which stressed the *qualifications* needed by young people. More recently this has changed. Employers are now more concerned about the KIND of youngster who applies for a job, than what their academic attainments may be. One large company states publicly that it is more concerned with *attitudes*, *personality* and *interests* of young applicants than with their CSEs, O levels or A levels. There is evidence that this employer point of view is on the increase; because if young people's attitudes are right, employers expect to carry out job-skill training more successfully.

In most industries, technological change is very rapid. New jobs appear, other older ones cease to exist. Young employees therefore should be adaptable to change, and be prepared to train so as to become multi-skilled. Employers may then more readily transfer employees from one task to another within the company as needs arise.

There is a wide range of jobs available

a) Distribution

Level of entry	Career ladder	Training, education and planned experience	
Entrant with no academic qualifications	Trainee sales assistant Sales assistant First sales	Induction (all entrants) Company knowledge Job skills and knowledge Planned experience	General Certificate in Distribution
O-level entrant	Sales assistant Section head Asst dept manager Asst sales manager Asst branch manager	Job skills and knowledge Supervisory skills and knowledge Introduction to basic management principles Planned experience	National Distribution Certificate
A-level entrant	Dept manager Sales manager Branch manager	Job skills and knowledge Management principles and practice Planned experience	Certificate in Distributive Management Principles* HND Business Studies (Distribution)*
Graduate entrant	Branch manager Area manager Shops inspector Buyer Sales manager	Job skills and knowledge Further management training Planned experience	Diploma in Management Studies*
	General manager Director	Updating in management skills and techniques	Short courses as appropriate

*Or appropriate trade-based courses

b) Engineering

Trainee designation/ Job level	Entry qualifications for training	Training course normally followed	Typical job opportunities
Junior operator	Academic standard slightly below that for craft trainee	Day-release for one year minimum	Semi-skilled machinist or assembler, inspector etc.
Craft trainee	Minimum 3 subjects CSE grade 3 (maths grade 1 or 2)	First-year full-time off-the-job training Day-release up to age 20	Skilled machinist, sheet-metal worker, fitter, toolmaker, inspector, etc.
Technician trainee	No direct entry Recruited as craft trainees with 1 or 2 O-levels	Transferred to C&G technicians' course or TEC in second year	Draughtsman, technical inspector, experimental technician, technical clerk, estimator, supervisor, etc.
Technician engineer aged 16	Minimum 4 O-level passes grade C, including maths, physics and English	1st year – full-time Engineering Practice part I and ONC/TEC 2nd year – ONC block-release followed by HNC or HND/TEC	Design draughtsman, work-study engineer, process-planning engineer, production-control engineer, instrumentation-development engineer, technical sales engineer, quality-control engineer, service engineer, technical buyer, technical author, standards engineer, supervisor, etc.
aged 18	Minimum 5 GCE passes, to include maths and physics at A-level and English at O-level	1st year – full time EP I and HND block/TEC 2nd year – TEC/HND block or degree course	
Graduate engineer trainee aged 18	Minimum of 2 A-levels including maths and physics, preferably grade A or B	TEC/HND plus Chartered Engineering Institute pt 2 or BSc (Engineering) plus approved practical and objective training	Design engineer, project engineer, electronics engineer, applications engineer, industrial engineer, etc.

A training session for staff at a store: they are learning company policy and about the goods they sell

New proposals

While it would be foolish to make too many assumptions about the future, it seems that certain changes in education and training for young people are likely to be made.

(i) As before, those aged 16 may opt to continue full-time education at school or in college, following A level courses, for example.

(ii) Other young people may accept a technician or craft apprenticeship. This is likely to be 'performance-based' in the future, rather than being 'time-served'. In other words, once you have reached a required standard, you are regarded as qualified, or able to begin a higher level course, rather than spending months or years carrying out the tasks before becoming officially qualified. These courses may well be set up by BEC or TEC (see p. 76).

(iii) You may enter work below apprentice level, and be required to complete at least a year's training, along with an associated element of further education.

(iv) You may not initially be able to find a position with an employer immediately on leaving school, but may have an opportunity to work within or outside your own community on a voluntary basis, and be able to take up a placement with an employer as soon as a training opportunity becomes available. This alternative also may have an opportunity for further education as part of the programme.

(v) Some young people may decide to opt out and make no effort to find a training placement with an employer, nor to contribute to their community to make life in general better for people.

In addition, some young people in groups (i)-(iv), or even (v), may be offered an opportunity to follow a period of residential experience away from their own locality. Such experiences offer exciting and

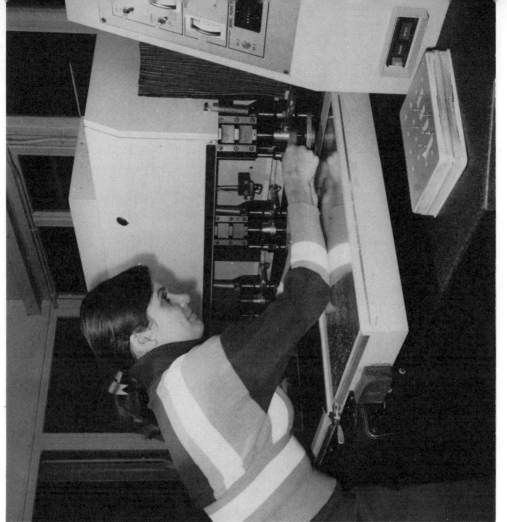

Precision control in the manufacture of printed circuit boards

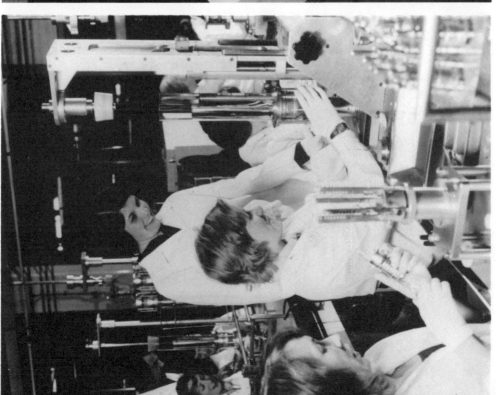

Supervising the production of television camera tube assembly

c) Motor manufacturing

School achievements	Training schemes	Age	Education and training programme	Job prospects
CSE: Mathematics, English Language, physics or a science, plus 1 other subject, preferably woodwork or metalwork	Craft	16	1st year 2nd year 3rd year 4th year City and Guilds courses Basic off-the-job training Module and specialist training	Toolmaker Motor-vehicle fitter Welder Maintenance fitter Electrician Pattern maker Sheet-metal worker Inspector Other skilled areas
GCE O-level grade C minimum or CSE Grade 1: mathematics, English language, physics plus 1 other related subject	Engineering technician	16/17	Technician Education Certificate courses Basic off-the-job training General and objective training	Draughtsman: jig and tool, body, layout, transmission, chassis, electrical, engine-design Laboratory technician Experimental engineer Quality engineer Sales/service engineer Industrial engineer
GCE O-level grade C minimum or CSE Grade 1: Mathematics, English Language, plus 2 other subjects	Business technician	16/17	Business Education Certificate courses or National Certificate in Business Studies General and Objective Training	Sales Purchasing Production and material control
GCE A-level: mathematics, physics; GCE O-level grade C minimum: English language, plus 4 other subjects	Engineering student	18/19	Degree courses at selected universities and polytechnics General and Objective Training	Design engineer Development engineer Production engineer Quality engineer Systems analyst Other specialist areas
GCE A-level: 2 subjects; GCE O-level grade C minimum: English language and mathematics, plus 3 other subjects	Business student	18/19	Degree or professional courses at selected universities and polytechnics General and objective training	Finance Sales Purchasing Systems Marketing Production and material control

enjoyable opportunities to extend your self-image and develop not only self confidence, but also many other aspects of yourself.

It seems that, at the time of writing this section, those young people who find themselves in groups (i)-(iv) above may receive a national grant during the first year after leaving compulsory education, and that those in group (v) may receive a reduced grant or no grant. Certainly, employers will have the opportunity to assess the potential of, and train young people, who themselves will have a chance to explore which are their most appropriate occupational areas during their first year post school, without actually appearing on the employer's payroll.

All this will be the probable outcome from the government document, issued in mid-1981, called *A New Training Initiative* (NII). The same paper strongly recommends that there shall be continued opportunity for adult employees to retrain as the needs of industry arise. Therefore YOU must make sure that YOU make the effort to obtain the *best available advice and guidance* to help you decide which pathway is the right one for you.

Whether or not you enter paid employment immediately on leaving school or college, or even if you have already left, there are a number of areas of competence which you should try to develop as well as your specific education/training qualifications.

These are known as 'work skills' rather than specific 'job skills'. If you acquire the skills listed below you will be not only a valued employee, or colleague, but also be enabled to perform as a true adult in other peoples' eyes, and be a competent problem-solving person both at work and outside the workplace.

- taking initiatives, and recognising where they exist
- being responsible for yourself and towards others
- co-operating with people, being able to be a member of a team
- able to accept and follow instructions
- capable of asking the right questions in an appropriate manner

- showing self-confidence, self-awareness and self-discipline
- able to persevere and complete a task
- able to plan the use of time and materials
- taking decisions and solving problems
- able to communicate accurately, and to listen attentively
- recognising the ability and strengths and problems of others as well as your own
- having an adaptable and flexible attitude
- developing a pleasant and helpful manner
- becoming a 'giving' or 'contributor', not just a 'taker'

Finally, your attitude to *retraining* is important. Industry is changing rapidly, and needs people who are *continually* useful. The idea that you need retraining *does not* mean that you are no good at your job, but that the job itself has changed, or ceased to exist, and therefore a programme of training is necessary to enable you to cope with this change.

Work experience - in the food hall of a department store

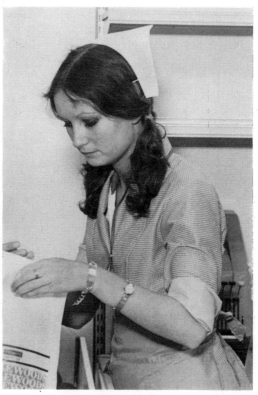

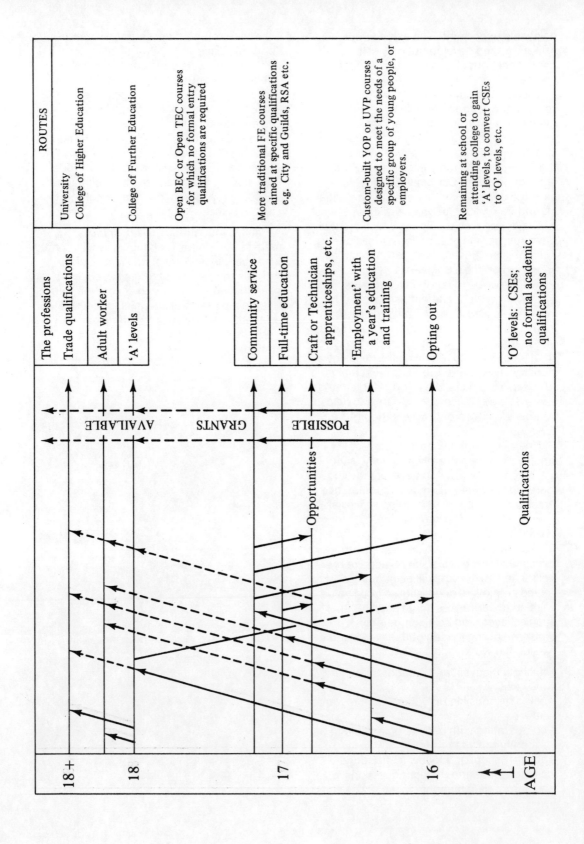

ROUTES

University
College of Higher Education

College of Further Education

Open BEC or Open TEC courses for which no formal entry qualifications are required

More traditional FE courses aimed at specific qualifications e.g. City and Guilds, RSA etc.

Custom-built YOP or UVP courses designed to meet the needs of a specific group of young people, or employers.

Remaining at school or attending college to gain 'A' levels, to convert CSEs to 'O' levels, etc.

The professions
Trade qualifications

Adult worker

'A' levels

Community service

Full-time education

Craft or Technician apprenticeships, etc.

'Employment' with a year's education and training

Opting out

'O' levels: CSEs; no formal academic qualifications

GRANTS AVAILABLE

POSSIBLE

Opportunities

Qualifications

AGE

18+

18

17

16

3.3 How can I tell?

Exercise 3

If you feel you have made up your mind, or reasonably so, what job you would like, copy out the table below and answer each question in the middle column of the table, and write 'yes', 'no', or 'don't mind' in the right-hand column. Look at these answers and, when you have finished, consider carefully how you feel. Do you need to change your mind or find out more about the job before you make any final decision?

Job satisfaction

This is rather difficult to describe. So many situations can provide it. A craftsman may get a great deal of pleasure from using his skill and seeing the results of his work. A teacher will be very pleased at the successes achieved by young people in school. Even a supermarket shelf-filler may enjoy seeing all the shelves neatly filled and tidily stacked.

Exercise 4

What satisfaction do you feel you would get from the job you are at present interested in doing? Name three different kinds.

Of course, there may be no job which offers you all you want, and as you become older your ideas and needs will change. And remember, jobs which exist

The job	Answer	Does this suit me?
Mainly outside or mainly indoors?		
Moving around or remaining fairly stationary?		
Hot, cold or comfortably warm?		
Clean or dirty workplace?		
Clean or dirty job?		
Dangerous or not unusually so?		
Noisy or reasonably quiet?		
Smelly or not?		
Well paid, badly paid, reasonably paid?		
Good or poor promotion prospects?		
Secure or insecure?		
Long, short or non-existent training?		
Is the industry or business strike-ridden?		
Do I have any weaknesses preventing me doing this job?		
Have I got the entry qualifications?		
Any weekend or evening work?		
Away from home occasionally? Never? For long periods?		
Will doing the job well give me pleasure?		
Will others respect me for it?		
Is it routine or variable work?		
Will I be supervised or left alone?		
Will I supervise others, or eventually so?		
How much annual holiday?		
Can I take it when I like?		
Large or small firm or business?		
Wide or narrow age-range of employees?		

Job satisfaction is sometimes difficult to explain

now may not exist in ten or twenty years' time, and new jobs will appear. Forty years ago, for example, there was practically no plastics industry.

3.4 Range of opportunity and levels of entry

Tinker-tailor-soldier. . . . What will you be?

In this course you will be and/or have been looking very deeply at yourself. What kind of person are you? What are you good at? What can you not do? The task facing you is to try to match your strengths to a job. A careers teacher's task is not to *find* you a job, but to help you to decide what *kind of job* will suit your talents and skills, your abilities and your interests. It is *most important* that you know the kind of job to look for even if you have, for a time, to do a different job from the one you really want. You can then apply for the job you would really like when a suitable vacancy occurs.

There are 26 000 different jobs in Britain, and more than 25 million workers. How on earth can you choose? Luckily it is not as difficult as it seems. The following exercise will help you narrow the choice but bear in mind that you may grow to enjoy a job which at first seemed unattractive.

Exercise 5

What kinds of businesses and industries are there in your area? What jobs do these offer? What are your educational attainments? What are your special abilities? What is your choice?

Break down all the muddle of *possible* jobs into groups of *related* jobs. These can be split up still further into groups which need different qualifications for entry. Do you need A-levels, O-levels, CSEs or no exams at all?

Types of work

Most people do one of five kinds of work. The rest – one in twenty – enter literary, scientific or mathematical jobs. The five main types are

a) *active/outdoor:* driver, postman, vet, police officer, etc.;

b) *office:* typist, secretary, stores clerk, etc.;

c) *social (working with and for people):* nurse, receptionist, speech therapist, bus conductor, shop assistant, etc.;

d) *practical (making or repairing things):* jeweller, toy maker, TV engineer, machinist, car assembly worker, etc.;

e) *artistic:* florist, window-dresser, photographer, actor.

Exercise 6

Now copy out the table below. In the spaces, fill in as many jobs as you can think of, suitable for both males and females. Remember that some jobs may not require any examination passes, while others need very high qualifications.

Active/outdoor

Office

Social

Practical

Artistic

Qualifications required

If you have done the last piece of work thoughtfully you will see that some jobs require different training and qualifications from others. Workers exist at four different levels.

a) _Operatives:_ These people need little skill in their jobs. Their training takes only a short time. Such jobs include receptionist, road-sweeper, dustman, coil-winder, bus conductor, cleaner, small-machine operator and shop assistant. CSE and O-levels are not very often required, but such qualities as getting on with people, care, dexterity or strength may be necessary.

b) _Craftsmen:_ These are skilled people who have had several years' training. They may also have taken up an apprenticeship of three or four years. CSE grades 2-4 and sometimes one or two O-levels may be required. Craft jobs include nurse, laboratory assistant, mechanic and shorthand typist. Several years' further education is often required, leading to a qualification such as ONC, OND or BEC/TEC in the craft, for example in carpentry and plumbing.

c) _Technicians:_ These people have jobs needing a high level of technical or scientific knowledge. They undergo three or four years of further education and a fairly long training. Examples include toolmaker, laboratory technician, public health inspector, concert pianist and estate agent. Usually four or five O-levels are needed, and training leads to HNC and HND.

d) _Technologists:_ These are the most highly skilled professional people. They spend several years at a polytechnic or university or undergoing other professional training. A-levels are required as an entry qualification to training. Jobs include doctor, dentist, architect, lawyer, optician, engineer and meteorologist.

Examples of levels of skill in several industries

	Engineering	_Building_	_Medical care_	_Foodstuffs_
Technologist	Engineer	Architect	Doctor	Food technologist
Technician	Draughtsman	Surveyor	Lab. technician	Dietician
Craftsman	Toolmaker	Carpenter	Nurse	Baker
Operative	Machinist	Driver	Porter	Salesman

Exercise 7

With the help of material from the careers library and anything you can obtain from home or elsewhere, prepare tables for each main type of work (see exercise 6), showing jobs which require different levels of entry.

For example, here is part of a table for the 'practical' type of work:

Job	Level of entry
Sewing machinist	No examination; short training
Jeweller	CSE and full- or part-time further education leading to the City and Guilds Diploma in Arts and Design (Jewellery)
Baking technologist	4 O-levels, one in a science, and a two-year full-time technical college course leading to the National Baking Diploma

Exercise 8

On the chart below the types of work are written across the top, and the different qualifications needed to do the various jobs are down the side. Copy out the chart and using your own knowledge or by looking up information, fill in as many jobs as you can in each space.

3.5 'Signposts'

'Signposts' is a card index used in the careers library. Its purpose is to suggest careers which might interest you and to tell you where to look for information about them.

How to use 'Signposts'

The white occupation cards are divided into groups. At the front of each group is a buff-coloured card with questions about your interests. Read through all the buff cards first. If your answer is 'Yes' to any of the questions on a particular card, you should go back and look at the cards in that group. As you look through the cards, stand up on its end any card which describes an occupation you would like to know more about. Go through the cards you have left standing up, and make a note of the careers-library classification in the top right-hand corner and of the titles of the books on the back. Now go on to the careers library - but first put the cards back, making sure they are in their right places. (The white cards are all marked with a letter in the top-left-hand corner - this shows which group they belong to. Within each group all the cards are in alphabetical order.) There are not cards for every job, but if you are interested in a job not included in the index, ask your careers teacher about it.

The pink cards at the back list school subjects in which you might be interested,

	Active/Outdoor	Office	Social	Practical	Artistic
A					
O					
CSE					
Nil					

and careers and higher-education courses that have a connection with each one.

'Signposts' is useful even if you already know what you want to do. If you look up your chosen career on the yellow card at the front of the box, it will tell you where to find the white occupation card which will indicate literature containing useful information on that career. You need to know as much as possible about your intended career. It is also a good idea to look at other cards in the group just to make sure you have not overlooked a career you might like even better.

The 'Signposts' system groups jobs into ten types, some jobs appearing in more than one list of job titles because they occur in more than one group. It also indicates levels of entry for training, some training details, personality and skill requirements and sources of further information. The main groupings are:

A   jobs involving the sciences;
B and D   helping and persuading people (organising jobs);
C   general service – jobs involving doing things for people;
E   literary jobs (those involving spoken or written language);
F   artistic jobs of a wide range;
G   jobs involving maths at various levels;
H   practical jobs, using hand and manipulative skills;
J   jobs concerned with plants and animals;
K   active/outdoor jobs.

There are two reasons for putting jobs into groups:
a) it makes it easier to store and get back information about them;
b) it helps a person to decide which career suits his or her abilities, ambition and personality.

Exercise 9

Copy out the table in the next column, and, in the space beneath each job, write which group (or groups) of those lettered A to K above you think it belongs to.

Chemist	Mechanic
Judge	Teacher
Dietician	Footballer
Clerk	Estate agent
Interpreter	Radiographer
Accountant	Lorry-driver
Butcher	Banker
Librarian	Plastics injection-moulder
Geologist	Doctor
Fireman	Forester
Beautician	Dressmaker
Window-dresser	Cook

3.6 Life-styles

Exercise 10

The jobs people do and the amounts they earn affect the way they live. Consider your ideas of a doctor, a shop assistant and a factory foreman. Copy out the chart overleaf and for each of them, say what you would imagine to be the most likely possibility for each aspect mentioned in the first column of the chart.

	Doctor	Shop assistant	Foreman
Length of job training			
Qualifications gained			
House lived in			
Length of working day			
Dress at work			
Make/size of car			
Wage/Salary			
Length of holidays			
Holiday resort			
Sports activities			
Home leisure interests			
Newspaper taken			
One or two cars			
Place where clothes are bought			
Membership of clubs and societies			
Add any other ideas of your own			

Find some means of discovering how correct your opinions are, and be prepared for some surprises!

3.7 Some questions

It is hoped that this unit has helped you to answer or at least discuss properly the following questions.

1 a) Is it necessary for the majority of people to work? Give reasons for your opinion.

b) What do *you* mean by 'work'?

c) What is *your* attitude towards people who do not have paid employment, for example old-age pensioners, the disabled, the unemployed, and those who *choose* not to work? (Remember that some people stay at home for such reasons as to look after children or invalid relatives.)

2 a) Can you say, in general terms and not tying yourself down too precisely, what kind of work you would like to do, and in which industry?

b) Work out your pathway, or route plan, for achieving this.

c) If your first choice is not available, what alternatives would be acceptable to you?

3 a) It is probable that in future less time will be spent in work (there may be a shorter working week, earlier retirement and more time off for study and retraining). What interests or hobbies would you like to develop, or do you feel drawn towards, to occupy what may be a greater amount of free time than you thought you would have?

b) If you had a pleasant job, but one which was easy or routine, what would you do about satisfying your wider interests?

c) Find examples of voluntary work, which gives some people great 'job satisfaction' but no monetary reward.

4 a) You cannot make simple assumptions about the type of work an organisation may offer. Think what are the main *ranges* of jobs offered by i) the AA, ii) a hospital authority, and iii) British Rail.

b) Look at a small company in your locality and find out what range of employment is necessary for it to carry on its business smoothly. (A one-man garage may have the same person repairing cars, dealing with customers, answering the telephone, doing the accounts and seeking new business.)

A young man in southern England made, as a hobby, a model of the Great Western Railway. He was offered £100 for it at an exhibition. This was accepted, so he had to make another model for himself. The one he sold went to America and soon he received orders for more. Sales are now worldwide. The young man employed twenty people by the time he was eighteen, and now has a flourishing business. What business could you, or a group of friends working together, set up? What enquiries would you have to make? What steps would you have to take?

Unit 4 Looking for work

Most young people do not regard themselves as grown-up until they are earning a wage and are financially independent of their parents. But jobs for young people may become more difficult to obtain; so it is essential that, if you want one, you must give yourself the very best chance of getting one.

This unit is designed to help you develop your 'job-getting' skills, and will indicate what employers are looking for. You must convey your eagerness to get a job, and show an employer reasons why he or she must regard you as a good investment. You will be in competition with many other people with a wide range of age and experience, so you must show that you have something special to offer – your enthusiasm, loyalty, youthfulness, interest and energy. Many young people do have these advantages, but fail to display them on an application form, in a letter or at an interview. Although in different places job opportunities will vary, it is always to your advantage to bear all these points in mind.

It would be unrealistic, however, to expect that every young person who really wants a job and who tries very hard to get one will succeed immediately on leaving school. Some may experience several months of unemployment first. If you know that you are doing all you can to obtain work, you should not feel guilty, ashamed or hesitant about obtaining social-security payments, which are intended to help you and your family during such a time. There are also, of course, many exciting opportunities for young people in this position, so make sure you ask your tutor or careers officer to give you details about the ones available in your area. An outline of some possible programmes is included in this unit. Remember that there will never be a shortage of work that needs or ought to be done, although there may be a shortage of paid employment.

Some time during this unit, obtain for yourself or ask your tutor to obtain a social-security benefit form, and ask your tutor to explain how to complete it.

4.1 Finding vacancies

Many young people will find jobs either on their own or with the help of their careers officers. Most job vacancies appear in sections of local and national newspapers – but you should read such advertisements with care. Most are informative and honest. Some are honest, but may not tell you all you wish to know. Others are frankly dubious, attractively worded and hinting at instant wealth if you accept the job – when quite often quite long unsocial hours may be needed to earn the necessary commission to top up a low basic wage.

Exercise 1

Look in newspapers and find an example of each of the types of advertisement mentioned above. Does each one tell you
a) the name, and address or telephone number, of the firm?
b) whom you should contact, and his or her status?
c) about hours, wages, and facilities like canteens and clubs?
d) the name of the job or the type of work you would be doing?
e) whether there is any age restriction?
f) what experience or qualifications you would need?
Point out any catches you can see. Some advertisements give a box number to which your application or enquiry should be sent; can you suggest any snags about using these? By the way, never send original documents, for example your birth certificate, to box numbers – always send copies; and never include money or stamped, addressed envelopes for replies. (Why not?)

'They told me the job provided steady work'

Where else can you find information about job opportunities?

a) Employment agencies

The sorts of jobs an agency has to offer are often shown on cards in its window. If it introduces you to a firm, it charges the firm a fee for having introduced you. *You* do not usually part with any money, although as a school-leaver you must have something special to offer an employer. However, it would be wise to check the arrangement.

Exercise 2a

Note the names of two agencies in your area.

b) Firms' notice boards

Many vacancies and opportunities for promotion are advertised both within a company and sometimes on its notice boards outside. Also read your local newspaper's classified advertisement section headed 'Situations Vacant'.

c) Magazines

Many newsagents, libraries and bookshops stock a large number of trade magazines. Your school or workplace may already take delivery of some of them. Ask your tutors, parents, friends and others which of these would be most useful to you.

Exercise 2b

Write down the names of any trade magazines which could help *you* in your search for a job.

d) Telephone advertising

This is still not widely used. It is a form of advertising where you dial a number and a recording lists several vacancies, including details of wages and whom to contact.

e) Friends and relations

'Knowing someone in the trade' is a useful method of finding a job. Be careful, however - someone else's choice of work may not be yours. Make sure you know all about the job before you take it on.

Exercise 2c

Ask your friends and relatives how they found their jobs.

f) Local college

Your local college of further education sometimes can find jobs for those who do well in their courses. But do not rely on this; and, before you attend a full-time course, find out what's going to happen to the students on the course *this* year.

g) Industrial Training Boards

See pp. 28-30.

4.2 Letters of application and application forms

If you apply by letter for a job, your letter should include
a) your own address;
b) the date;
c) the firm's address;
d) an opening sentence saying what job you are applying for;
e) a short paragraph giving your age and school, and saying what subjects you have studied and to what levels;

f) a second paragraph saying more about yourself – school duties, clubs, hobbies, interests, sports; and

g) a sentence at the end saying when you would be able to go for an interview if you were chosen as a possible employee.

Your letter will tell those who read it a great deal about you, so take a lot of care with it. Do it in rough first. For a medium-to-large firm, address your letter to the 'Personnel Officer' or 'Training Manager'; for a small-to-medium firm, address it to the 'Manager' or 'Managing Director'. For a commercial firm (that is, not a manufacturing business), address it the same way, or to the 'Branch Manager' if appropriate; for a hotel or shop which is owned by the person who runs it, send your letter to the 'Proprietor'. For the Civil Service, address your letter either to the Clerical Co-ordinator of the Civil Service in your region or to the Civil Service Commission in Basingstoke, Hampshire.

Start your letter with 'Dear Sir' or 'Dear Madam', and end it with 'Yours faithfully'; or, if you address the person by name, saying for example 'Dear Mr Robinson', end with 'Yours sincerely'. It will also help to print your name in capital letters below your signature.

Exercise 3

To whom would you address a letter in the following cases?
a) A butcher's shop;
b) a department store;
c) a factory;
d) a hotel;
e) a brewery;
f) a supermarket;
g) a hospital;
h) a large garage;
i) a café;
j) the local council;
k) a timber yard;
l) an insurance office;
m) a TV-rental firm;
n) a hairdressing salon;
o) a children's home.

Exercise 4

Choose an advertisement from your local newspaper, and write a letter of application for the job concerned.

Exercise 5

Ask your careers teacher to show you some good and poor letters of application. How many things can you see wrong with the poor ones?

Application forms

When a firm or other employer sends you an application form, remember you have only *one* form; fill it in very carefully with no mistakes. It is a good idea to do it in pencil first. Also *read* the form very carefully. It will probably ask for block letters (that is, capital letters) in some places. When you have completed it, *check it over* for *accuracy* and *spelling*. Like a letter, a form can tell those who read it a lot about you.

The application forms of some firms are more complicated than those of others. Fill in a fairly difficult form for practice. Ask your careers teacher about anything you do not understand.

You may be asked to name two or three *referees*. These are people whom the firm will write to or telephone to ask for information about you. You could name your head teacher, subject teacher, school head, tutor, church minister or youth-club leader, or any responsible person who knows you well. You should not name a relative or school-friend.

A *testimonial* is a letter, written by someone like the people named above, and given to you to send (in the original or copied) with your application.

Exercise 6

Here are application forms from two well-known British firms. Only their names have been changed. Make copies then try filling them out.

Metal Coils and Springs Ltd

Application for student or technician entry

Surname (block letters)

Forenames (block letters)

Date of birth   Age

If available please attach
a recent passport-type
photograph

Permanent address

Used since   Telephone no.

Address for correspondence

Used since   Telephone no.

Give any address outside UK used within last 3 years (except holidays), with dates

Place of birth   Nationality at birth   Present nationality

Surname at birth if different   If naturalised, give date

Mother's full name   Parent's present nationality

Mother's maiden name   Father's full name

Nationality at birth   Nationality at birth

Place of birth   Place of birth

Parents' present address if different from above

Used since (date)

(cont.)

Record any disability, accident, or serious illness

Intended date of leaving school   Date sought for start of training

Previous Employment, e.g. part-time or holiday jobs:
Name of organisation   Dates   Duties performed

School record:
Schools attended since age 13   From   To

Examinations completed and to be taken:

Exact subjects	Examining board	Month/ year	Level	Results and grades

Out-of-school activities:
Outline your hobbies, interests, spare-time activities; mention any offices held, also courses attended, awards gained

Name and postal address of present headmaster and school (last if you have left)

Are you prepared to live away from home?

Date   Signature

The Parson's Nose Chicken Packing Co. Ltd.

Application for employment

Any engagement entered into is subject to the following:
a) information given on this form being accurate; b) passing a medical examination; c) references proving satisfactory; d) joining the pension fund on 1 April following 6 months' service for men or on 1 April following 5 years' service for women, when proof of i) date of birth, and ii) marriage (where applicable), will be required.

Until conditions a), b) and c) have been fulfilled (but for a period not exceeding 6 weeks) employment may be instantly terminated. Thereafter, employment is terminable in accordance with your contract of employment. Condition d) applies only to full-time staff.

To be completed in block capitals:

1 Position applied for _____

   Surname _____ First names _____

   Home address _____

   _____

   Present address (if different from above) _____

   _____

   Date of birth _____ Married or single _____

   (For married women) Maiden name _____

   _____

2 Source of application, e.g. newspaper (give name), leaflet, window poster, etc.

   If recommended by a member of the staff, give branch or department _____

   Full name _____

   If you have worked for this company before give branch or department _____

   Position held _____ Dates from _____ to _____

   Reason for leaving _____

   _____

3 (For applicants under 18)

   Are you living with your parents, guardian or relative? _____

   If with a guardian or relative, give surname and initials _____

   Father's occupation _____

   (cont.)

49

Name and address of your last school _____

_____

Date started _____ Date left _____

_____

4 (Medical History)

i) Approximate height _____ ft _____ ins Approximate weight in stones _____

ii) Is your eyesight good in both eyes? _____ (Glasses, if worn, must be produced at

medical examination)

iii) Do you suffer or have you suffered from any of the following? Write 'Yes' or 'No'.

Varicose veins? _____ Foot trouble of any kind? _____

Discharging ears? _____ Skin trouble of any kind? _____

Any 'carrier' disease (e.g. typhoid or dysentery) _____

iv) Do you suffer from fits or blackouts? _____

v) Have you had any operation or suffered any serious accident or illness? _____

If so give brief particulars _____

vi) If you have had a chest X-ray, state date _____ Result _____

vii) If you are a disabled person, state (a) registered number _____

b) Nature of disability _____

Applicant's signature _____

Exercise 7

Discuss this with a partner. How many mistakes can you find? What conclusions would you come to if you were the employer and received a form like this one?

The Clockwork Mouse Co. Ltd

Post applied for ~~Pickler~~ Packer

Full name (surname first) (block capitals) Arthur. C. Bottomley

Address 135 Torbay ~~Road~~ Ave.

Date of birth 30ᵗʰ June

Place of birth Branston Infirmery

Passes at O level (French) (English)

Passes at CSE level ↓ ↓ Geography + First Aid Certificate

Give 2 referees Mr + Mrs Bottomley, address above.

(I hope I get this job because I have always been interested in
Welding and Soldering)

4.3 Interviews

There are several reasons for holding interviews. The general point is that the employer meets you and you meet him, so he learns more about you than appears on any application form or in any letter. It often occurs that, even if your qualifications are a little lower than hoped for, an interview persuades the employer to take you on - perhaps because of your bright, pleasant personality, or your keenness to do a good job.

Points to remember:

a) be on time - even a little early;

b) be neat, smart and clean;

c) be pleasant, and try to explain answers to questions rather than just saying yes or no;

d) try to find out about the firm before you go, and, if an opportunity arises, ask to be shown around;

e) take relevant documents or records with you - reports, certificates, etc.

Exercise 8

Sometimes an interviewer will have a checklist. Look at the assessment form below. How might it be used to select employees for different jobs?

Confidential

ASSESSMENT FORM

Job title

Candidate

Please complete in full

The ratings are as follows:

A is excellent   B is above average   C is average

D is below average   E is exceptionally poor

	Rating	Notes
1 Physique, health, and appearance:		
height	A B C D E	
build	A B C D E	
hearing	A B C D E	
eyesight	A B C D E	
general health	A B C D E	
looks	A B C D E	
grooming	A B C D E	
dress	A B C D E	
voice	A B C D E	

(cont.)

	Rating	Notes

2 Attainments:

   general education   A B C D E

   job training   A B C D E

   job experience   A B C D E

3 General intelligence:

   tests   A B C D E

   general reasoning ability   A B C D E

4 Special aptitudes:

   mechanical   A B C D E

   manual dexterity   A B C D E

   skill with words   A B C D E

   skill with figures   A B C D E

   artistic ability   A B C D E

   musical ability   A B C D E

5 Interests:

   intellectual   A B C D E

   practical constructional   A B C D E

   physically active   A B C D E

   social   A B C D E

   aesthetic   A B C D E

(*cont.*)

6 Disposition:

acceptability   A   B   C   D   E

leadership   A   B   C   D   E

stability   A   B   C   D   E

self-reliance   A   B   C   D   E

---

7 Circumstances:

age   A   B   C   D   E

dependents   A   B   C   D   E

mobility   A   B   C   D   E

domicile   A   B   C   D   E

other points   A   B   C   D   E

              A   B   C   D   E

              A   B   C   D   E

Additional information and overall comments

Signature of interviewer ....

Date ....

Prepare sensibly for an
interview

Certain qualities will be essential if a person is to get a particular job; others may be desirable but not absolutely necessary. The table below gives an example of this.

Employee Specification: Sales Manager's Secretary

Attribute:	Essential:	Desirable:
Physical make-up	minimum age 22; neat appearance; well-spoken; average good health;	minimum age 25; smart; attractive;
Attainments	English language at O-level; RSA Shorthand/typist's Cert. stage II (shorthand 80 w.p.m., typing 50 w.p.m.); 4 years' experience as shorthand/ typist and/or junior secretary;	2 other subjects at O-level; stage III (shorthand 100 w.p.m., typing 60 w.p.m.); 5 years' experience;
General Intelligence	sufficient to learn the job quickly; suitable behaviour for the position;	
Special Aptitudes		skill with figures; skill with words;
Interests		social; physically active;
Disposition	stable; calm under pressure; confident, self-reliant;	cheerful;
Circumstances	current driving licence; able to be away from home occasionally; confident, self-reliant.	

At an interview you will usually have an opportunity to ask questions – for example, about training, wages, overtime, trade-union membership or holidays. Prepare some at home and, if the information is not given you during the interview, ask them.

Exercise 9

Look at the picture opposite. Discuss, with a partner or in a group, who may and who may not get the job. Be prepared to give reasons for your comments.

4.4 Using the telephone

A few points to remember:
a) dial carefully, not hurriedly, taking your finger round to the stop;
b) speak clearly without shouting;
c) spell words, especially names, which are not clear;
d) be prepared to jot down information such as directions, times, etc;
e) if you are using a public telephone, make sure you have enough money for the call;
f) if *you* made the call, and *you* get cut off, *you* make the call again;
g) use people's names if you can - people often love the sound of their own names.

Test your knowledge and your ability to express yourself clearly by describing to a partner:
a) the 'pay' ('insert money') tone.
b) the ringing-out tone which indicates that your call has reached its destination;
c) the 'engaged' tone, indicating that the telephone is in use at the number you have dialled;
d) the 'number unobtainable' tone (this may be due to re-allocation of numbers, or perhaps your contact has moved).

Exercise 10

Read the following exchange of remarks and, either in group discussion or on your own, list the mistakes in it. It would be interesting to rewrite this conversation correctly and if possible to tape-record it. Hearing your own voice on tape can sometimes be rather a shock!

Receptionist Good morning, Clockwork Mouse Company.
Fred Can I apply for the job?
Receptionist Who would you like to speak to?
Fred Mr What's-his-name, the bloke who wrote the advert.

Receptionist I'll get Mr Robinson, the training manager, for you.

Mr Robinson Training department.

Fred Oh, it's about the advert for the job.

Mr Robinson Which job do you mean? We have a number of vacancies.

Fred A packer, I think it was, or something like that.

Mr Robinson Are you unemployed, or still at school?

Fred I haven't got a job and I'm leaving soon, in a fortnight.

Mr Robinson So you're still at school. Which one is it?

Fred The comprehensive.

Mr Robinson There are eight comprehensive schools in this town.

Fred Oh, I thought there were only six. I go to the one by the police station.

Mr Robinson There are at least two police stations.

Fred Oh, I mean the one by the post office next to the market – Brightbridge School.

Mr Robinson Why do you want a job in this factory?

Fred It's near home, so I needn't get up too early.

Mr Robinson Very well. If you give me your name and address I'll send you an application form, or if you prefer you can write to me giving the details of yourself and your school subjects. But I suggest you buy an alarm clock before you do so.

Fred Thanks a lot. I will. Ta-ta.

While the conversation may have amused you, Fred made some very stupid mistakes because he could not communicate properly. He probably did not listen carefully to what was required. Certainly he did not give accurate information.

4.5 Communicating accurately

One interesting way of discovering whether you can communicate accurately in conversation is to try the following exercise.

Exercise 11

Draw an accurate diagram on a sheet of paper, but do not let your partner see it. Then, standing back to back, describe it, little by little, in the form of spoken instructions, according to which partner will re-draw the diagram on paper. (You must not explain what you mean in a long-drawn-out way – just give short instructions. Also, your partner may not ask you any questions.) Then see how alike your drawings are.

Use your own diagram, but here is an example.

Repeat the exercise, but this time your partner can ask *one* question after hearing any instructions he does not understand.

Then you try to draw from your partner's instructions.

Another exercise is the same except that you can converse freely. However, you must not show the drawing to your partner *or indicate whether it is being drawn correctly.*

What have you found out from doing these exercises?

Exercise 12

If you can obtain and use a tape-recorder, try this more difficult exercise. Your tutor will probably check several points with you afterwards. It might also be fun to give your tape to a friend or relative to type, and ask for comments about it!

You are a buyer. Tape a letter to your secretary, which she must type while you are out the following day visiting another firm. Be sure to remember that your audio-typist will need not only the letter itself but full information about it. Copies are needed for your file, the sales manager's secretary and the marketing department.

This is the letter to be dictated:
To the Chief Buyer of Plastex Ltd,
Barton Road, Rexton, Roxall.

Dear Mr Simmonds,

Thank you for your order for 500m of
heavy-gauge PVC. This will be delivered by our
company transport on Thursday 2 October to
your stores, in a consignment of 5 rolls of
100m, each roll being 2m in width.

The invoice and delivery note will be handed
in to your purchasing department by our driver.

I should like to bring to your notice the
following new product, Heavy Duty Plastolene,
which is suitable for swimming-pool and
garden-pond liners. Wholesale prices are as
follows per 100m roll:

Width	Red	Beige	Black	Grey
2m	£27.50	£26.00	£28.00	£25.00
3m	£30.00	£39.00	£32.00	£37.00
4m	£45.00	£42.00	£46.00	£40.00

Please note that there is a 10% discount on
all orders over £120.00, provided the account is
settled within 28 days.

Yours sincerely
(p.p.) Alex Roberts
Sales Supervisor

4.6 Job tests

As well as interviews, some employers may
want to give you their own tests.

Exercise 13

In one city, the maths teacher and
employers met to discuss the range of
maths needed over several industries. Just
one example of each type of calculation is
given in the following test. Remember that
not *all* employers require *all* this range of
ability, but the questions give a fair
indication of what might be needed by
school-leavers whose ambitions lie at
operative, craftsman and technician levels.

1. Place in order of size, with the smallest
   first, 1000, 0.07, 40, 0.009, 576.
2. Work out a) $137+4094$, b) $236-75$, c)
   46×7, d) $666 \div 9$.
3. Work out a) $2+3 \times 4$, b) $5 \times (7-3)$.
4. Work out a) $14.09+376.4$, b)
   $321.7-68.09$, c) $\frac{3}{16}+\frac{1}{4}$, d) $3\frac{1}{4}-\frac{11}{16}$.
5. Write a) $\frac{3}{8}$ as a decimal, and b) 0.85
   as a fraction.
6. Work out a) 3.7×0.27, b) $10.01 \div 0.13$.
7. Work out a) $1\frac{3}{5} \times 2\frac{1}{2}$, b) $2\frac{1}{4} \div \frac{3}{4}$.
8. Express a) 76 inches in feet and inches, b)
   46.9 cm in mm.
9. Round a) 23.6597 to one decimal place, b)
   60.5384 to three significant figures.
10. a) Find the average (arithmetic mean) of
    13, 6, 25, 17, 16.
    b) Six apprentices have ages 17 yrs 10 mo.,
    17 yrs 6 mo., 17 yrs 3 mo., 17 yrs 5 mo.,
    17 yrs 8 mo., 17 yrs 10 mo. Find their
    average age.
11. a) What is 27% of £2?
    b) Write $\frac{5}{8}$ as a percentage.
    c) What percentage of 1 kg is 245 g?
    d) Write 75% as a fraction.
12. Work out a) $4-9$, b) $-3-12$, c)
    $+6-(-5)$, d) $(+3) \times (-5)$, e)
    $(-8) \times (-6)$, f) $(-49) \div (+7)$, g) $(-10)^2$, h)
    $(-3)^3$.
13. Measure the length of the line in mm.

    _____

14. Find the area of A in cm^2, and find the
    volume of B in cm^3.

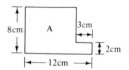

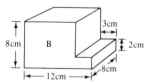

15 The two lines marked with arrows are parallel. Write down the size of angles a, b, c and d.

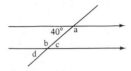

16 Pick out the correct answer:
476,000 in standard form is
a) 4.76×10^3, b) 47.6×10^4,
c) 4.76×10^5, d) 4.76×10^6.

17 Work out $(2 \times 10^3) \times (3 \times 10^{-2}) \div (1.5 \times 10^2)$, and give your answer in standard form.

In questions 18 to 22 all you have to do is to estimate the answer. *Do as little working-out as possible.* Pick out the nearest answer from those given.

18 37.9×52.3 is approximately 0.02, 20, 200, 2,000, 200,000.

19 $27 \div 0.52$ is approximately 0.5, 1.4, 5, 14, 50, 140.

20 A cubic foot holds about $6\frac{1}{4}$ gallons, so a water tank 4 ft by 5 ft by 4 ft will hold about 50 gall., 120 gall., 500 gall., 1200 gall., 5000 gall.

21 A single-track railway is 15 km long. The sleepers are about 75 cm apart, so the total number of sleepers is about 1000, 2000, 4000, 10,000, 20,000, 40,000.

22 Building bricks are roughly 8 inches long, 4 inches wide and $2\frac{1}{2}$ inches thick. Roughly how many bricks would there be in a stack 20 ft long, 5 ft wide and 3 ft 4 in high – 600, 700, 800, 6000, 7000, 8000, 60,000, 70,000, 80,000?

23 Work out the circumference of a circle of diameter 7 cm. (Take π as $3\frac{1}{7}$.)

24 Work out the area of a circle of radius 10 cm. (Take π as 3.142.)

25 Work out the volume of a cylinder of height 5 in and radius 10 in. (Take π as 3.142.)

26 A cylindrical metal rod has a circumference of 12 cm. It is mounted in a lathe and rotates at 100 revolutions per minute. Calculate the surface speed in metres per minute.

27 The dry ingredients of concrete are cement, sand and gravel mixed in the ratio 1 : 2 : 3.
a) How many kg of each are there in 300 kg of dry mix?
b) How much cement and gravel is needed to mix with 4 cwt sand?

28 Solve the equations a) $4x + 3 = 15$
b) $3y + 6 = 5y - 2$.

29 Make s the subject of the formula $v^2 \div u^2 + 2as$.

30 The total surface area of a circular cylinder is given by the formula $a = 2\pi r(r + h)$, where A is the area, r is the radius of the ends and h the height of the cylinder. Calculate the total surface area of a cylinder with radius 5 cm and height 15 cm. (Take π as 3.142.)

31 Using tables, work out the square roots of a) 7.29 b) 144,000.

32 Use logarithms to work out a) 47.96×0.0384 b) $679.2 \div 4.763$.

33 In a right-angled triangle the two shorter sides are 9 cm and 12 cm long. Calculate the length of the hypotenuse and the size of the smallest angle.

34 Calculate the lengths x and y shown on the diagram below.

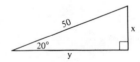

Here are examples of three other kinds of tests which may be given. Try them, writing the answers out.

1 a) i) *Accuracy*
What errors, if any, exist in the copy, compared with the original?
Original:
Mrs Jane Scott Reading, Berks   £731.10
Mr Edward Hill Doncaster, Yorks   £432.11
Copy:
Miss Jane Scot Reading, Bucks   £731.01
Mr Edward Hell Doncaster, Yorks   £432.11

ii) *Error location*

Add horizontally and vertically. Spot errors.

			Totals				Totals
4	3	9	16	5	11	4	20
5	8	2	14	8	7	10	18
7	8	6	17	7	9	13	29
Totals 16	14	17	47	13	27	27	67

b) **i)** *English grammar*

Correct the following if wrong:

1 Where was you going?

2 I brought a pair of shoes for £2.50.

3 I am sending only one letter.

ii) *Vocabulary*

Underline the word meaning the *same* as the word in capitals:

TIRED —late, climb, heavy, weary, slow.

iii) *Relationships*

Picture is to frame as diamond is to glass, ruby, setting, finger, money.

c) Non-verbal reasoning

1 If the cogwheel labelled **A** rotates in the direction shown by the arrow, in which direction will wheels **B**, **C** and **D** rotate, if **A** drives all the wheels round?

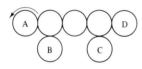

2 Fill in the blank square in each set.

4.7 Unemployment and redundancy

Very few people want to be unemployed, but unfortunately it happens far more than we wish. There will be some people who, however hard they try, cannot get work for some time after leaving school. Others will lose their jobs after only a short period in work - either a) through being made redundant, perhaps on a 'last in, first out' basis, or b) through being sacked: for continual lateness, a lot of absence without good reason, shoddy work, disobeying the firm's rules, stealing or fighting. They may find it hard to start again.

But all is not doom and gloom.

First of all, the best plan is to go and see your careers officer if you are under eighteen, or, if you are over eighteen, to either see him or her or call at the local offices of the Department of Employment. Explain your problem frankly and honestly. It is these people's task to help you find a job, or another job. Also call at your nearest Job Centre.

Secondly, most towns and cities organise job-creation schemes. The opportunities vary from place to place, but your careers office will tell you about openings in your area. Here are a few examples of such schemes.

a) Star or Gateway courses

These are for school-leavers who have been unemployed for six weeks or more. You spend thirteen weeks either doing vocational training, or doing a job with day-release for such training at a college of further education. It is hoped that at the end of this time a job will be found for you. During your training you will be paid *about* £20 per week, and some fares if you travel considerable distances.

b) Industrial Skills courses

These are sometimes offered by firms not using all their equipment. The government pays back the firm any wages they pay you.

c) Community Industry

This means jobs created by the council, or even individuals, which help the local community in some way. Each job lasts for one year, but you may leave it at any time if a better job comes your way. Such work includes woodwork and repairs, painting and decorating old people's homes, renovating old buildings, assistance in hospitals doing various jobs, library work, etc. You must be eighteen in order to be considered. Pay is £20-25 per week.

d) Work Preparation

This is a twelve-week course for those who, either because of a personality problem or because of a genuine fear of going to work, need a special introduction to the world of work. The course is part-time in college and part-time in a firm.

e) Recruitment of School Leavers (RSL) scheme

For inclusion in this scheme you must a) already be on a Star course and be prepared to start full-time work shortly after completing it; or b) already be on a Community Industry project; or c) have left school and been on the unemployed register for at least six weeks; or d) be under twenty and prepared to start *full-time* work.

f) Industrial Training Board schemes (see pp. 28—30)

The government is prepared to pay certain firms to take on more young people than they in fact need, provided that these young people undergo training and are allowed day-release for further education courses. This money is used to pay the trainee and all further-education course fees.

g) Job Centres

In every town there is a Job Centre in which all types of vacancies for all kinds of people are displayed. Go in, browse around, and talk to the assistants who will be glad to help you. This service is free of charge but do remember that it is up to you to approach the staff and not their job to approach you.

In getting the best out of these schemes three pieces of advice are useful.

a) Keep in touch with your careers office.

b) Keep a log or diary of *all* your achievements during the last one or two years at school, to show employers at interviews.

c) Do something for yourself. Get up and *go*! If you want to work for a particular firm, visit or ring asking for an interview. *Ask* if there are any vacancies and make it clear how good you are, and what a loss the firm would suffer if they did not employ you!

It is possible that despite all that, you will still be unemployed. If so, try looking at it this way.

a) You now have time to do something you have always longed to do. What is it? You may never get an opportunity like this again.

b) Someone living only a few doors or streets away may really need your help. He or she may be young or old, and ill or afraid. Just think how many people volunteer to help others, without pay. Why not become one of them for a while? You may find great pleasure in this.

The Holland Report (work-experience programmes)

In 1977 the Manpower Services Commission, an arm of the Department of Employment, produced under the guidance of Mr Geoffrey Holland a very important report. It suggested that, at sixteen, school-leavers should be regarded as trainees, and should be entitled to an allowance over and above dole money provided they undertake a course of further education, training or assessment, and work experience or work preparation. It is possible that a maintenance allowance will also be made for those remaining at school to do higher education programmes, such as A-levels.

There are quite a number of different patterns of training or assessment under this scheme. Mainly these involve both work experience and further education. It is hoped that those undertaking them will

Work experience in a commercial firm

Trainees being presented with their UVP certificate at
the end of their course

shortly end up in permanent jobs. Full details of all this can be obtained from your careers office. The only qualification is that you must have been continuously unemployed for six weeks after leaving school before you become eligible to take advantage of the scheme.

Exercise 14

Everybody is a person of great worth, no matter whether they are clever or not. Try to recognise what you are good at. Then try in some way to make yourself *better than anyone else* at that special skill. It may be cooking, cleaning, painting, reading, shopping, driving, playing a game, following a sport, repairing things, typing, knitting, gardening, baby-sitting, organising - or *anything*! To help you spot such skills, copy out and fill in the following table as honestly as you can.

	School subjects, hobbies, or spare-time interests which answer any of the descriptions in the left-hand column
Finding out how things work	
Office-type work	
Helping others	
Persuading others to do things	
Making or repairing anything	
Any kind of artistic work	
Work requiring physical strength	
Any kind of work with animals or plants	

Exercise 15

On a copy of the following list, add a tick or a cross according to whether or not you would be willing to help others voluntarily in the way mentioned. Be honest. After all, no two people are exactly alike, or have exactly the same abilities and/or interests.

Babysitting
Looking after schoolchildren
Shopping
Handling other people's money
Doing housework
Cooking
Running errands
Gardening
Reading to old people
Making clothes for others or for yourself
Painting and decorating
Writing letters for others
Playing games
Cleaning cars
Caring for animals

Now make your personal list of ways in which you are able or willing to help others in *any* way, and a list of any other activities you could undertake (including things you could make or do for self-employment). Compare your list with those of others in a small group, and see if you can come up with new ideas through co-operating with each other.

Exercise 16

What would *you* do if any of the following happened to you?

a) You could find no vacancies near where you live for the job you would like.

b) You had no job because you had made little or no effort to get one.

c) You needed to pass four examination subjects to be accepted for your job, and you only passed in three.

d) Your parents moved house, and there were no courses in any college in the town you moved to which gave the kind of training you require.

e) An accident caused you permanent injury – say to your hand – so you could no longer do the job you hoped for.

f) The firm you were going to join closed down.

4.8 Some questions

This unit should have helped you to tackle the following questions.

1 What positive plans could you make, for yourself or in co-operation with your friends, to use your free time fruitfully, usefully and enjoyably in the event of having more of it than you expected?

2 a) What advice and help could you give someone about to leave school and wanting to get a job?

b) What advice could you give to such a person who had failed to get work and was becoming depressed or concerned?

3 What plans would you make if the latter happened to you?

4 What new decisions will you have to make, when you get your first job, about

a) money management?

b) job-keeping?

c) making friends?

5 How do you think that being at work will change your present life-style?

6 a) Do you agree that the invention of machinery enables people to lead more enjoyable lives? (Perhaps thinking of the past twenty years, weekly working hours and holidays may help you to form your arguments and opinions.)

b) What effects do you think further development of machinery and increasing technology will have on people's lives in the next ten years?

Unit 5 **Starting work**

In units 1 to 4 we have looked at the opportunities for school leavers to get paid jobs or find other work. This unit deals with the problems which you will meet when starting work and taking your place in the world as an adult.

Every adult needs to know about such matters as National Insurance and income tax, and the rules, regulations and formalities connected with working life. Once you have left school there may be no help available to understand these matters except through chance contacts. If you find yourself in difficulties and need the help of an official, he may *or may not* advise you as to your most advantageous immediate action or entitlement.

You may find this unit the most difficult to deal with, but for these reasons it is hoped that you will make the effort to understand clearly at least the most important parts of it.

5.1 Some jargon and its explanation

Exercise 1

One of the first documents you will be given upon starting a job will be your contract of employment. The one shown here is from a well-known firm, and it is part of what they call their 'Starting Advice'. Look carefully at all the information there. Is there anything else you would like included? Ask your tutor about any points on the document which are not clear.

The Clockwork Mouse Co. Ltd, Torbay Road, Northam

Starting Advice   Date

Name _____

You have been provisionally accepted for employment initially as a

. . . .

(subsequent job changes may arise from transfer and/or promotion, etc.)

at a wage/salary of _____

to commence work on _____ the _____

Please report to the _____ at _____

Previous service _____ Holiday _____

Address of branch _____

It is important that you have your National Insurance card and income-tax form P45 with you when you start work.

Any queries should be addressed to the place of work shown above.

Confirmation of employment depends on the conditions specified on your form of application being fulfilled. For a period not exceeding 6 weeks, employment may be instantly terminated. Thereafter employment is terminable in accordance with the written particulars of your contract of employment set out below.

Contract of employment:

Date of issue _____

To _____ _____ From The Clockwork Mouse Co. Ltd

Your employment commences on _____

Payment As above, paid weekly/4-weekly; if 4-weekly, payment is by bank transfer. For further details covering any shift and overtime entitlement, etc., see documents which are available at your place of work.

Hours of work Your normal hours of work are _____ a week. Daily working hours vary within departments. For further details of schedules see documents available at your place of work.

Holidays For entitlement and method of calculation see notice board and/or documents available at your place of work.

Payment during sickness or injury For details of payment and regulations see documents available at your place of work.

Pensions The Company has not contracted out of the government graduated pension scheme, and in addition operates a pension and life assurance scheme, membership of which is a condition of employment for full-time staff where eligible. Further details are available in a booklet obtainable at your place of work.

Notice of termination of employment: For full-time employees (i.e. all employees who work, or are normally expected to work, 21 hours a week or more) all notices of termination will be given in writing as follows:

	Employee to give	The Clockwork Mouse Co. Ltd to give employee				
Completed service	Over 6 weeks	6 weeks – 2 years	2 –5 yrs	5 –10 yrs	10 –15 yrs	Over 15 yrs
Weekly paid staff	1 week	1	2	4	6	8
4-weekly paid staff	4 weeks	4	4	4	6	8

For part-time employees, i.e. those who work, or are normally expected to work, less than 21 hours per week, notice of termination is one week.

Rights under the Industrial Relations Act 1971 The company recognises the employees' rights in respect of trade-union membership and activities as laid down by section 5 of the Industrial Relations Act 1971. For further details see documents available at your place of work.

Grievance procedure Details of your grievance procedure are obtainable from your Departmental Head (or Branch Manager) and from documents available at your place of work in the Office Managers Office or Personnel Office.

Any change in these terms and conditions will be indicated in the appropriate documents not more than one month after any such change.

It is also important when starting work that you ask or are told what special clothes or headgear to wear. Usually the firm will supply these. If you have to buy your own, the firm will often pay part of the cost and an income-tax allowance will be available; but make sure you buy good-quality things.

Exercise 2

Make a list of six jobs, each of which require special clothing, and say what that clothing is. Then make a list of five jobs needing special headgear. Say what it would be and the reason why it would be needed.

Exercise 3

During your first few days at work most firms provide an induction programme. This should tell you all you need to know - about the firm's rules, about safety and about fire precautions - and outline your training programme. The document shown below requires the trainee to sign in recognition that all this has been done. The firm also sign, to indicate that they have done their part properly. Of course, procedures vary from firm to firm, but the general pattern will be the same. Look carefully at this 'branch induction' sheet. Is there anything further you would wish to be included?

The Clockwork Mouse Co. Ltd

Branch Induction

Branch _____ Trainee _____

Date of engagement _____

Subject	Date	Signed
Personnel officer:		
Company history	_____	_____
Role of the branch personnel officer (BPO)	_____	_____
Salary and wage structure; appraisals; promotion	_____	_____
Appraisal scheme	_____	_____
Reporting sickness; special card re infectious diseases	_____	_____
Branch telephone no.	_____	_____
Sickness payment	_____	_____
Holiday entitlement	_____	_____
Hours of work; Saturday off/overtime	_____	_____
Pension scheme	_____	_____
Disciplinary procedure	_____	_____
Staff interviews: manager and BPO	_____	_____
Trainee to sign rule sheet	_____	_____
Clocking in/out procedure	_____	_____
Protective clothing	_____	_____
Lockers and keys	_____	_____
Smoking rules	_____	_____
Canteen facilities and meal breaks	_____	_____

	Date	Signed
Notice-boards	_____	_____
Further education	_____	_____
Hygiene and appearance: hair, etc.	_____	_____
Deputy manager:		
Training; checklist system; multi-skills	_____	_____
Staff orders; non-serving of relations and friends	_____	_____
Branch security	_____	_____
Fire procedures: tour of branch	_____	_____
Safety/first aid	_____	_____
Use of internal telephones —restricted use of external phones	_____	_____
Use of lifts	_____	_____
Manual lifting techniques	_____	_____

_____Manager

_____Trainee

_____Date

Another company's induction procedure

'The object of good induction training is to obtain the best performance from a new employee as soon as possible. The benefits to everyone are considerable. Labour turnover and absenteeism are reduced —recruiting new labour is expensive. New employees become productive more quickly. Better employer-employee relations develop. The firm improves its image and attracts good-quality labour. New employees are relieved of the anxiety that follows a change of job.'

How to use the checklist

Most sections should be covered within the first few days: 1, 2, 3 and 5 on the first day. 6 and 7 may be done in small groups within the first month. Put a tick in each ☐ when point is understood by trainee.

Responsibility for induction:
personnel —training —safety —departmental
superintendent.

Remember how you would feel on the
first day in a new job.

On morning of first day   Personnel 1
- ☐ obtain P45 form
- ☐ explain rates of pay (basic, overtime, bonuses, etc.)
- ☐ hours of work and breaks
- ☐ how, when and where paid
- ☐ check holiday commitments
- ☐ social and recreational facilities
- ☐ locker issue
- ☐ prepare contract of employment
- ☐ ....
- ☐ ....

Explain rules and procedure   Personnel 2
- ☐ explain wages/salary slip
- ☐ obtain signature for deductions
- ☐ time-recording and keeping
- ☐ late for work —effect on pay
- ☐ absence —sick notes
- ☐ arranging time off
- ☐ annual holiday arrangements
- ☐ company rules and discipline
- ☐ canteen facilities
- ☐ transport and parking
- ☐ personal problems —who can help

Departmental induction   3
- ☐ foreman welcomes newcomer to department; show toilet, washroom, cloakroom.
- ☐ no-smoking rules
- ☐ fire drill, nearest emergency exit
- ☐ other safety procedures
- ☐ tea and meal-breaks
- ☐ emphasise need for punctuality
- ☐ importance of tidiness
- ☐ report to supervisor after absence
- ☐ effects of absence on rest of department
- ☐ overtime availability and arrangements
- ☐ if you sleep in, come to work —don't take the day off
- ☐ introduce to other members of department and ensure that they will help the newcomer to settle down; explain each person's job

- ☐ explain purpose and organisation of job training to be given
- ☐ lifting and handling instructions
- ☐ ....
- ☐ ....

General works safety   Safety officer 4
- ☐ works rules
- ☐ Factories/Offices Act
- ☐ protective clothing
- ☐ lost time is wasteful
- ☐ smoking regulations
- ☐ fire drill
- ☐ encourage tidiness
- ☐ safety policy
- ☐ ....

Health and Welfare   Safety officer 5
- ☐ arrange medical, if needed
- ☐ first-aid facilities
- ☐ accident reporting
- ☐ factory health hazards
- ☐ shoe/overall purchasing
- ☐ ....
- ☐ ....
- ☐ ....
- ☐ ....

Health and welfare   Safety officer 5
- ☐ company products and markets
- ☐ company history
- ☐ company organisation
- ☐ tour of works, introduce to foremen, describe role of each department, point out toilets, exits, first-aid room

Industrial relations   Training officer 6
- ☐ trade-union membership
- ☐ introduce to union representative HSA fund
- ☐ education, training, promotion and transfer
- ☐ savings scheme

I have received induction training, as
shown on this checklist

Signature of new employee   Date

Supervisor's comments   Initials
Any follow-up to induction required?

Job training will cover.........   Date
Anything else..................

Exercise 4

Many firms will give you a job description or job specification. This is really a list of your duties and responsibilities. Look at the examples below, and then try to make up a job description yourself for any job of your choice. You may be able to obtain information and help from your careers library.

Job specification

Job title: Secretary

Duties:

1   takes dictation of letters, inter-office memoranda, reports, etc., and transcribes on typewriter;
2   transcribes from all types of dictating machines;
3   types reports, lists, minutes, etc., and cuts stencils when necessary;
4   opens and sorts incoming mail, and files correspondence;
5   answers telephone and takes messages;
6   answers routine correspondence in the absence of supervisor, within prescribed limits;
7   contacts personally and by telephone directors, executives and their secretaries to deliver messages and reports;
8   receives director's visitors;
9   keeps engagement book;
10   makes travel and hotel arrangements;
11   collects salaries for the department;
12   keeps codes and other references and records up-to-date;
13   requisitions stationery;
14   carries out general clerical work;
15   works under immediate supervision.

Job description

Department: *Warehouse typing pool*
Job title: Junior copy typist

Date:

Major function: to produce typed order forms.

Working procedure: types out orders from written information on to form X12 and returns them to clerk for checking and signing; types standard letters to customers about 4 times weekly.

Working conditions: works in a pool of twelve typists under normal office conditions.

Equipment used: standard typewriter.

Job knowledge: typing and ability to read and write.

Responsibility: no responsibility for work of others; works under immediate supervision at all times.

Contacts: other typists, supervisor, and clerks for whom he/she types orders.

Education and experience: secondary modern school; typing speed 30 w.p.m.

Job description: Sales assistant
Responsible to: *Department Manager*
Function: *to sell goods and give satisfactory customer service*

Tasks:
to sell as many goods as possible;
to give a high standard of service to our customers;
to give accurate information to customers about our goods;
to know how to sell and demonstrate goods;
to know about our most recent advertising and window-displays;
to deal with orders and enquiries by telephone;
to encourage customers' self-selection;
to rotate stocks and clean fixtures;

to carry out correct price-ticketing;

to deal with documents regarding deliveries and missing stock;

to undertake stock checking;

to set up displays of our goods for both self-service and display purposes;

to be aware of the Trade Descriptions Act;

to deal with cash, cheques and usual till procedures;

to pack and despatch goods as required;

to maintain sales records and inform workrooms of jobs;

to deal with customer complaints;

to be aware of stock security and methods of pilfering;

to ensure security of cash;

to take care of new staff.

5.2 Appraisal

A job appraisal is in many ways rather like a school report. Look at the example below. Once or twice a year a look may be taken at how well you are doing your job. Your promotion may well depend on this process. If you have not been trusted to get on with your work on your own, do not be too upset – your supervisor will also be appraised by his or her boss!

The Clockwork Mouse Co. Ltd
Staff Training Department

Department: *Sales*

Appraisal of junior packers

In accordance with the Distributive Industry Training Board requirements I have appraised:

Name _____   Position held _____

Dept/branch/section _____   For the year ending _____

Basis of appraisal: Measure of performance:

	A	B	C	D
Timekeeping	____	____	____	____
Relations with staff	____	____	____	____
Packing & warehousing efficiency	____	____	____	____
Promotion recommendation	____	____	____	____

Training recommended in respect of present position _____

Special training for future promotion _____

Signed_____Foreman_____Packer_____

5.3 Structure of firms

Every office, factory and firm has its own orderly structure. The bigger the employer, the more complicated the set-up. Here is an example:

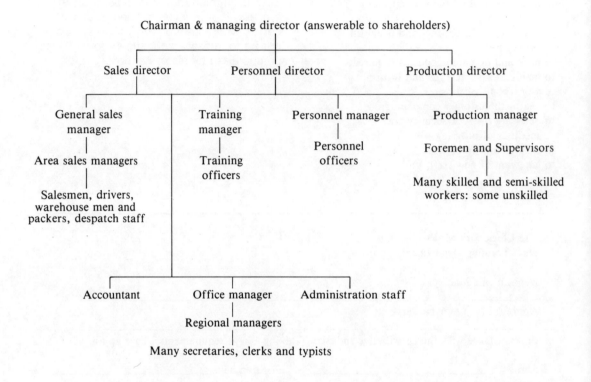

Chairman & managing director (answerable to shareholders)

Sales director   Personnel director   Production director

General sales manager — Training manager — Personnel manager — Production manager

Area sales managers — Training officers — Personnel officers — Foremen and Supervisors

Salesmen, drivers, warehouse men and packers, despatch staff — Many skilled and semi-skilled workers: some unskilled

Accountant   Office manager   Administration staff

Regional managers

Many secretaries, clerks and typists

It is important to know who is your boss

You can see that it is important to know who is *your* boss, and where *you* fit in.

Exercise 5

Just a thought – if you find you can't get on with some people at work, ask yourself whether it is really their fault, or perhaps yours. Think of six reasons why people might not be able to get on with each other at work.

5.4 Money matters

Wages

When you earn your own money, instead of depending on your parents for pocket-

70

money, how will your wages be decided? Some people have their wages determined by *collective bargaining*. What does this mean? Such people include clerical workers, shop workers, textile workers and electricians. Other workers, for example hotel workers, laundry workers and hairdressers, have their wages decided by Wages Councils. Here are some expressions that crop up when money is being discussed.

Flat rate   by law, the least you can be paid for any job. However, the employer may offer more if certain conditions are met.

Commission   An added payment based on how much you sell, made in some retail trades.

Piecework   Work paid for according to the number of items you make in a given time. The more you make, the more your pay.

Salary   An amount paid in some jobs over a year; usually paid in twelve equal monthly sums.

Wages   Your pay-packet. In some industries workers are paid in several ways - and at several time-intervals: sometimes by the hour, sometimes by the day and sometimes by the week.

Money matters

Overtime   Money paid for all time worked above the agreed 'week' of, say, forty hours. Each extra hour or day will be paid at perhaps 1¼ to 1½ times the normal rate.

Above basic rate   Usually paid for especially difficult jobs, unsocial hours, shift work and special tools (such as a mechanic or hairdresser may require).

Increments   The usual increases in pay each year for the first few years. These are often paid on your birthday, but in some careers (for example, in teaching) they are paid each April, regardless of when your birthday is. At present the full adult rate for most jobs is payable when you are twenty. For example: if the full rate is £50, then at sixteen you might earn £20, or 40%; at seventeen £25, or 50%; at eighteen and nineteen, £30 and £40, or 60% and 80%; and at twenty the full rate, or 100%.

Bonuses   Additions to the basic rate for such things as good attendance at work, good timekeeping and producing at least an agreed minimum output per day or week. Bonuses are paid for many contributions, like these, made by employees to the continued success of the organisation concerned.

To ensure that you are paid the proper wage, inspectors visit factories at any time, and always, in the case of any complaint, check the books. The trade unions also have the responsibility to see that proper rates are paid.

Deductions from pay (stoppages)

Most people have some of their pay stopped. Some stoppages are compulsory, and others - such as savings - voluntary.

a) Income tax

This is money you pay to the government to cover such things as defence, law enforcement, education, roads, railways, social services and industrial growth. The amount you pay depends upon how much you earn. Your teacher will tell you the rates, or tell you how to find them out. You will have a 'tax coding'. Single people have a letter L after the code number, and married couples the letter H. If you do not wish your employer to know whether or not you are married, the letter T will be used. Your code number is the amount of allowances without the 'units' number; for example, if your allowances are £500 your code is 50. Your income tax is stopped out of your pay by your employer, and so is called PAYE, for Pay As You Earn. Ask to see your parents' or tutor's 'PAYE Coding Guide'.

b) National insurance

This again will be explained by your tutor, and you will be told the rates for different people. This money ('contributions') goes to pay for the items below.

i) *Sickness benefit:* pay when you are away from work ill.

ii) *Unemployment benefit (dole money):* money paid when you cannot find work.

iii) *Family allowance:* payment to help feed and clothe your children.

iv) *Retirement pensions:* money paid to elderly people who have stopped work (at present this is paid to women over sixty and men over sixty-five).

v) *Maternity benefit:* payment to help with the extra cost of having a baby.

vi) *Death benefit:* money to help with funeral expenses.

vii) *National Health Service:* this provides such things as doctors' wages, hospitals and clinics of all kinds, welfare workers, health visitors and the cost of prescriptions and dentists' fees, and pays for several other things. (You may have to pay something towards medicines, spectacles and false teeth.)

Ask your parents where your Department of Health and Social Security office is.

c) Additional stoppages

1   Many firms, and all professional and government organisations, run a *pension fund.* You pay into this from the day you start work until the day you retire; contributions are usually a percentage of your earnings. You will then, after retirement, be paid each week or month a pension from this fund as well as the National Insurance retirement pension. Your contributions are stopped out of your pay by your employer, and the scheme is sometimes called *superannuation.*

2   Also, in many jobs you will be expected or required to be a member of a union. Your union fees, or subscriptions, will be collected by a union official.

3   Some firms run *savings schemes,* and you may, if you wish, ask them to save a certain amount each week or each month by stopping it out of your pay. You can of course draw this money out at any time.

4   Often firms have many social activities and sports facilities, and while they usually pay for most of the facilities themselves you may be expected to pay a little towards the cost; of course, the more clubs you join the more you pay. But it might be as little as 10p or 20p per club per week.

Gross pay is pay before stoppages. *Net pay* is what you take home.

Ask your careers office for any more information about all this.

Works/clock no.	Name	Date
Tax code	Gross pay	Net pay
Nat. Ins.	Income tax	Overtime
Pension	Savings	Other deductions

Above is a typical pay-slip. Look at the information given on it. Sometimes pay slips are even more complicated. Ask your careers teacher what other information is given on teachers' pay-slips.

Exercise 6

1   What is a form P45? What is a form P60?

2   Although you can save through most employers, you can also save through the

National Savings Bank (once called the Post Office Savings Bank), a building society, a bank current account, a bank deposit account, stocks and shares, and Savings Certificates. Find out or discuss the advantages and disadvantages of these methods. Which might suit you best now?

3   If a person who smoked ten cigarettes a day stopped smoking, how much would he or she save in a year if the cigarettes cost 30p for ten?

4   You may be paid in cash, by giro cheque or by banker's cheque, or your pay may be paid directly into your bank account. In the last method of payment, on each pay-day you would only receive a pay-slip. Discuss in groups or with your careers teacher which method you prefer, giving your reasons.

5   Which is the higher rate of pay, £650 per year or £12.30 per week?

6   Which is the higher rate of pay, £56.10 per month or £13.40 per week?

7   What do you think would be the rates of pay for an office worker at the ages of seventeen, eighteen and nineteen, if he or she earns £25.00 per week at sixteen and the adult rate at twenty is £50.00?

8   If you earn £1250 per year and have tax allowances of £600, and you are single, what would be your tax code? How much tax would you pay?

9   What is the tax code for a single person earning £2000 per year at the proper single person's allowance? Work out the code for a married man earning £3000 a year. How much tax would each person pay in the year?

10   Work out the tax code, allowances, and tax paid in a year by a married man with three children, one aged ten, one fourteen, and one seventeen and still at school, if the man earns £4000 per year.

11   What is the tax code for and tax paid by a blind lady if she earns £2500 per year, and has her daughter helping in the home?

12   Draw a blank pay-slip. Fill it in as fully as possible for a self-employed male hairdresser who earns £60 per week.

13   A single woman aged 20, who works at a local factory and earns £55 per week, saves £2 per week in the factory savings

Most people have some pay stopped

scheme. She pays 20p per week to the factory social club fund and 50p per week as her union subscription. How much is her gross pay per year? How much is her net pay per year? What are her total stoppages for the year? Draw and fill in her pay-slip.

14   Assuming you live at home, your take-home pay is £30 per week and that you work in the city centre, prepare a neat table of what you think your weekly budget might be.

Budgeting

What do you believe 'pocket-money' to mean? How much pocket-money do you get? Exactly what do you spend it on? How do you decide how to spend it if you do not have enough to buy all you would like? The sharing-out of your money so that most of what you want you get in time, if not at once, is called *budgeting*.

When you start work you will end up with your net pay. What are you going to do with it? What will you have to find from it? Consider some of the following points.

You are now one of the wage-earners in your home; should you give part of your pay to help run it? If you live in a council house, there will be the rent, electricity, fuel and food all to be found, at something like £45 per week for a family of three or four. If your parents are buying their house with a *mortgage*, should you help to repay this? What is a mortgage? And what about *rates*? What are rates? How does your town or district spend the money it collects from house-owners, shops and firms?

Ask your parents if they can help you make out a chart showing where their money goes. In addition, remember expenses like fares to work, meals during the day, make-up, footwear, clothes, hobbies, cigarettes, records, magazines, etc. If you do not live at home you will also be required to pay your share towards the cost of a flat or wherever else you live. How much do you think this would be? Would it be cheaper than living 'at home'?

Hire-purchase

Young people who cannot afford to pay the cash price for items they need or would like often buy them on HP - sometimes called the 'never-never' because it seems as though the things you buy will never be paid for. If you are under eighteen you must find an adult or adults - say your parents - to act as guarantor(s); they must be able to help you if you find you cannot manage the *repayments* yourself - otherwise the hire-purchase company may decide to take the article back. You must remember that goods are always more expensive when bought in this way, so it is better to pay *cash* if you can.

On HP young people might buy, for example, a car, a cooker, furniture, a record-player, clothes or a carpet. *But be careful!* It is easy to buy so much in this way that you do not have enough to live on after paying the HP bills.

Credit cards are another way of obtaining money to buy goods before you can pay for them in full. Find out about these and how to use them (Barclaycard and Access are the two best-known). Get a leaflet from your local bank. How can you open a bank account and obtain a cheque book? What are the advantages of doing so?

5.5 Further education and training

Nearly all jobs except the least skilled require some training, and the training period will naturally vary in length according to the amount of education and skill you need to acquire.

By *higher education* we usually mean attending school at sixth-form level and proceeding to a college of education, a college of higher education, a university or a polytechnic. *Further education* is usually obtained at a college of further education, art and design, or technology, and usually runs parallel to training inside a firm.

There are considerable differences between FE, HE and school. Colleges of further education work longer hours, sometimes into the evening. You would meet quite a wide age-range of students, who might be studying a wide range of subjects. Some students would be full-time, some part-time; some attending voluntarily, some because employers required them to do so. They would come from a wider geographical area than those at your school. You might have to provide your own stationery and other materials, but you would usually find sports, social and canteen facilities on the campus.

In higher education you must be responsible for working on your own;

All jobs require some sort of training

74

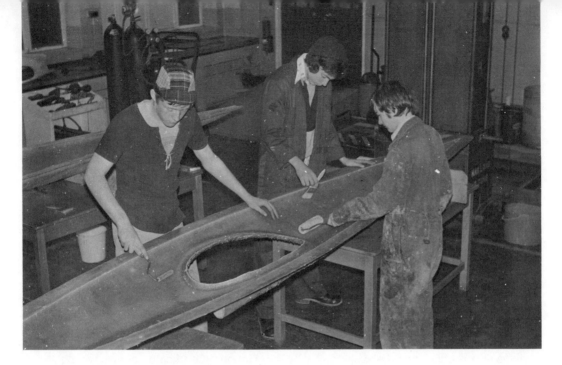

Off-the-job training in an industrial training school

indeed on some days you might have no
lectures, lessons or practicals. You would
normally have to achieve quite high
educational standards in order to be
accepted as a student. Holidays are longer
even than school holidays, and there are
no set periods for physical education or RE
(you would join clubs of your own choice
in these fields). Normally you would get a
grant from your local authority to help pay
for your books, lodgings and so on. You
would study your limited number of
subjects in great depth; and, unless it were
outrageous, your behaviour would be your
own affair.

It might help if some of the words used
in FE and HE were explained.

On-the-job training This is given by your
employer at your place of employment.

Off-the-job training This takes place away
from work. In some industries the whole
of the first year of apprentice training
may take place in a college of FE.

Day-release Usually this refers to one day
a week, over a period of one to three
years, which is spent at a college of FE
as part of your training, and for which
you are paid.

Block release

Block-release This is continuous off-the-
job study for a number of weeks, say
eight to ten, at a college or similar place,
paid for by your employer.

Sandwich course This is a period of
training which takes place in a series of
blocks, usually alternating between
employer and college or polytechnic.
The length of the blocks in a sandwich

course can vary, but it is usually six months, one year or two years. A sandwich course usually leads to your obtaining a degree, often in engineering. Now for some of the more important sets of initials.

C & G   City and Guilds of London Institute. C & G courses, usually for a craftsman's certificate, can be obtained by day- or block-release. The C & G Foundation Course is run in many schools and is usually based upon some aspect of job interest.

RSA   Royal Society of Arts, usually concerned with awards for commercial and secretarial training.

ONC   Ordinary National Certificate. Studied for in a college of FE on day-release or block-release by trainee technicians, or business or managerial studies. You often need O-levels to qualify for the course.

OND   Ordinary National Diploma. This is equivalent to A-level standard and covers a slightly fuller syllabus than ONC. It is acceptable as a qualification for a degree course.

HNC   Higher National Certificate. This requires ONC or an A-level to qualify for entry, and lasts for two to three years. Often this is the highest qualification a college of FE awards; it represents a very high technical standard, and forms a degree entrance qualification.

HND   Higher National Diploma. This is similar in standard to a pass degree, and is usually studied at polytechnics, though some colleges of FE may run such courses, too.

TEC and BEC   Technical Education Council and Business Education Council (see p.2). These are quite new organisations whose standards are similar to those of ONC, OND, HNC, etc., but with a different and modern syllabus structure. Eventually the National Certificate courses will be replaced by these.

GTS   Group Training Scheme. Often small employers cannot afford their own training schools or workshops, so a number of employers together contribute

Training in a technical college. These young people are not yet actively involved in production

towards setting up a training school used by all members of the group. The training officers will then recruit and train young people for all the member companies.

5.6 Trade unions

What are trade unions?

Unions are groups of working people who join together to talk to employers about wages and conditions at work, instead of talking individually to them. Because it speaks for everybody, a union can get a better deal for each worker than he could get by arguing with the employer on his own.

Problems and difficulties aren't invented by trade unions. They arise at work because, in any organisation, things don't always run smoothly. Unions exist to sort out workers' problems by getting round the table with employers.

Some issues, such as wages and holidays, need more than simple discussion. They have to be bargained about. This is because for the employer, higher wages mean higher costs for the business, but for the workers low wages mean they can't afford to buy the things they want. So there is a lot of argument, and eventually a compromise is reached which both sides accept.

Whatever job you will be doing, there will be a union for you to join. In nearly all firms of any size, the majority of workers belong to trade unions. There are more than ten million trade unionists - men and women - in Britain today.

Among the people you are likely to meet soon after you start your first job will be members of the union at your place of work. Experienced union members will help answer your questions about your work, and about what the union does.

Who decides how much I'm to be paid?

For almost all jobs, discussions about rates of pay take place between employers and union leaders covering whole industries. The aim is to agree on a basic level of pay for everyone in the country doing the same job. For instance, there are national rates of pay for all schoolteachers, all shop assistants and all postmen.

But in many jobs the national rate provides only part of the pay-packet. It is added to by further payments agreed on in talks in the individual factory, shop or office.

Pay for overtime or piece-work may also be decided in discussions between the union and the employer in the workplace. There may be special payments, too, where the workers and their union co-operate with the employer to improve working methods.

Overtime

There are laws preventing young people from being employed for very long hours, or at night. But you may be asked to work some overtime. Now, overtime may make sense from the employer's point of view - it helps the company deal quickly with a big order, for instance. But, for you, work in the evenings or on Saturdays means less time for what you enjoy doing - going out and seeing your friends, for example.

Unions are out to shorten working hours. And they are seeking improvements in the basic rates of pay, so that workers don't have to work overtime to take home a decent wage. Where overtime *is* worked, the union can insist that workers' wishes are taken into account, as far as possible, in deciding who does it, when they do it, and what they are paid for it.

Health and safety

Things often happen at work which affect workers' health, safety, or comfort. For instance, you may have to use dangerous equipment, or to work with harmful substances. The workplace may be very noisy. It may get hot and stuffy - or uncomfortably cold. An important job of the union at work is to make sure the employer deals promptly with any risks to the safety or health of its workers.

Thanks to trade-union pressure on governments, there are laws laying down basic standards of health and safety at work. But unions argue that the law doesn't go far enough. They are pressing for improvements - for regulations to ban noisy machines, for instance.

How does the union bargain?

The union normally sets out its demands - say for a pay rise, or for more holidays - in writing. These form a 'claim'. It then asks the employer for a meeting to discuss the claim. This leads to a round of talks - *negotiations* - between the two sides. During the negotiations, the employer will usually make an *offer* - that is, it will say how far it is prepared to go to meet the workers' claim. The union reports the offer to its members, who decide whether to accept it.

Rarely will a union be offered everything it has asked for. Both sides in the negotiations will be willing to compromise - to reach an agreement which both accept as reasonable. Occasionally, however, a union may make so little progress in negotiations that it may ask its members to stop work, to show how strongly they feel on the issue, and to show the employer its business will suffer if it maintains an unyielding attitude. If workers in a factory go on strike, the union may support them with strike pay until a settlement is reached.

But, although strikers are always in the news, the average worker loses only a few hours a year through strikes - less time than he loses because of the common cold. Millions of trade unionists have never been on strike. The overwhelming majority of problems are solved by arguing them out around the table.

Consulting the members

Unions were formed by workers themselves, to help get better pay and conditions at work. And the union can only do what the members want it to do. Union leaders are not commanders-in-chief, ordering their members about. They spend a lot of time consulting members - finding out what they think the unions should do.

When negotiations are happening in a single workplace, it is easy for the union to find out what members think of the employer's offer. A meeting can be held at work - in working hours, in the lunch hour, or after work.

When negotiations involve members in other firms - for instance, on the pay claim covering a whole industry - consulting members is more difficult. The employers' offer may be considered at local union meetings, or a ballot of all members may be held.

But whatever decision is taken - whether to accept an offer, or reject it - it must meet the wishes of the members. Unless members are happy with an agreement, the agreement can't work smoothly.

Other union activities

Unions run all kinds of courses for their members - for instance, on work problems, and on how government policies affect your job and your standard of living.

Unions work hard to help keep down the number of accidents in industry. But if you should be unlucky enough to be injured at work, the union can give you skilled legal advice. And, if necessary, it will take up the case for compensation for you in court.

Many unions run convalescent homes and benevolent funds. In most cases, too, they are affiliated to trades councils (bodies of people representing different trade unions in a particular place), and to the Labour Party at local and national level.

What does joining involve?

All union members must pay a regular subscription to the union's funds. Subscriptions vary, but for young workers they are usually only a few pence a week.

Joining the union gives you the right to

the union's support in all kinds of problems which may arise at work. It entitles you, too, to any cash or other benefits provided by the union. It gives you the right to go to union meetings, and to vote in union elections. You will have a full chance to speak and vote on questions about what the union should do.

Many decisions are taken by a simple vote of the members concerned. Sometimes you may be outvoted on a question; but, if the vote goes against you, you will be expected to go along with the decision of the majority. Unions place great stress on unity – because, when workers are divided, the employer may try to set one group off against another to get its own way.

Every union has a printed book of rules. The rule book gives information about subscriptions and any cash benefits. It generally also sets out how union officers are chosen, and how members decide what the union should do.

How are unions organised?

The shop steward

Union members at the workplace elect their own spokesman, generally known as a 'shop steward'. The steward is not paid for his union work, and he usually carries on at his normal job. He speaks for union members on all the problems which need to be dealt with on the spot – questions of safety or overtime arrangements, for instance. But he is not only a spokesman, he is a one-man advice bureau as well. He spends a great deal of his time helping the people who have elected him with their individual problems – for example, sorting out the details of their pay slips, with all their deductions and additions. An official report, by the Royal Commission on Trade Unions in 1968, saw his role as 'oiling the wheels' in day-to-day dealings between workers and employers.

The branch

Union members belong to branches, which meet regularly near members' homes or places of work. At branch meetings

members can have a say in what the union does, and how it is run. They elect their own branch secretary, chairman and committee. They choose delegates to attend the union's national conference, usually held once a year. Ideas on many issues that matter to working people are put forward by the members in their branches. Proposals then go to the conference, where the members' own delegates decide by a democratic vote whether to accept them or not. If they are accepted, they become part of the union's official point of view.

National organisation

Each union has a national executive committee, which acts on behalf of all the union's members. The committee is elected either at the union's national conference or by a ballot of the members.

The TUC

There are well over a hundred trade unions, each covering a different industry or job. The unions come together in a body called the Trades Union Congress – the TUC. The TUC's main job is to put forward a trade-union point of view on things which come up for decision by the government. For example, the TUC has pressed successfully for laws on factory safety and on equal pay.

An example of union structure

Annual conference:
the supreme policy-making
body of the union

↑

Executive council:
the authority between
annual conferences

↑

Area council:
the provincial
administrative unit

↑

Branch:
the basis

5.7 Rules and regulations: safety

The rules of different firms and employers vary slightly, but here are some of the safety rules you will find operating in most manufacturing companies:

General safety rules

1   Do not remove, or interfere with, any guard or safety device. If you have reason to think that it is defective, report it to your foreman or supervisor.
2   Report at once faulty machines or tools, or any conditions likely to cause an accident.
3   Avoid loose, flowing sleeves and ties and any other loose ends of clothing which catch in machinery. Never wear identity bracelets, finger-rings and similar types of personal jewellery.
4   If you have to work in oil or liquid, ask your supervisor to see that you are supplied with a barrier cream to avoid skin irritations.
5   A tidy place is a safe place. Play your part in avoiding accidents by keeping aisles, gangways and your own workplace clear and tidy.
6   Pay attention to *Warning Signs*. Look out for SMOKING PROHIBITED notices; there will be a particular fire hazard in these areas. Be careful to put out cigarettes and matches properly.
7   Report to First Aid for every injury, however slight.
8   Have foreign bodies removed from your eyes in First Aid. To allow a workmate to do it may cost you your sight.
9   Do not obstruct exits, fire equipment, safety equipment, switchboxes, etc.
10   Find out where the fire exits are, and where extinguishers are located.
11   Pile and stack material safely.
12   Horseplay, running, throwing, scuffling, etc., lead to accidents. Do not take part in them.
13   Do not crowd, run or scuffle downstairs. Try to keep one hand free for the handrail.
14   Wear sensible shoes. Safety shoes will protect your toes from injury and can be obtained through the company.

15   Never attempt to operate any equipment or machine unless you are familiar with its operation and have been authorised to do so.
16   Do not tamper with electrical equipment. If you find equipment out of order or damaged, report it immediately.
17   Learn the location of stretchers in your department. Learn to be able to render prompt assistance in the event of an emergency. Do not attempt to move a seriously injured person unless you have special training in first aid.
18   *If in doubt, ask.*

Offices do not usually seem to be especially dangerous places, but read through this set of rules on office safety and you will see just how wrong that assumption can be if a particularly careless person uses an office!

Office safety

1   *Filing cabinets*
Never have more than one drawer open at a time, and close it immediately you move away. When filling a four-drawer cabinet for the first time, start with the second drawer from the bottom; this will give weight to the cabinet and prevent it toppling over. Do not open drawers any wider than necessary.
2   *Guillotines*
These should be provided with guards to prevent finger access to the cutting zone. Never leave the arm of the machine in the air.

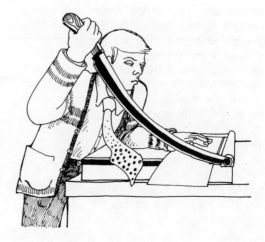

3 *Other cutting tools,* such as knives, razor-blades, scissors and paper-knives, all have sharp edges and can inflict serious injury. Razor-blades should only be used in a special holder and should not be left loose in drawers.

4 *Stapler*
Keep your fingers clear of the end when refilling. Staples should be fully pushed home so as not to leave the ends exposed.

5 *Pins and drawing-pins*
These can cause severe puncture wounds; pins should not be used for fastening papers together. Never keep drawing-pins loose in your desk drawer.

6 *Desk drawers*
Do not pull these out too far. Close them immediately after use.

7 *Typewriters*
On an electric typewriter, ensure the plug has been removed before going home and before cleaning. Typewriters are heavy objects; when carrying, the body of the machine, which is the heaviest part, should be against your stomach, with the keys away from you.

Switch off machines when not in use, unless manufacturer's instructions state otherwise.

8 *Electrical*
Remember, only authorised people should carry out electrical work. Never remove guards or covers from any machine unless you have been trained.

9 *Trailing cables* from telephones and electrical office apparatus - typewriters, calculating machines, dictaphones, electric fires, etc. - create a hazard. They should be kept to a minimum, and should never pass over walkways.

10 *Chairs*
Tilting chairs back is dangerous. Never use chairs or stools to gain additional height.

11 *Walking*
Many offices are covered with vinyl tiles, which become extremely slippery when wet; therefore, if any liquids are split they should be cleaned up immediately.

Platform-soled shoes are not designed for walking around an office.

Always walk, do not run, particularly up- and downstairs. When using stairs make sure you have a good hand-hold.

12 *Lifting and carrying*
Never attempt to lift objects that appear to be heavy or bulky. Make sure when carrying a load that it is not so high that you cannot see around or over it.

13 *Fire*
If you are a smoker it is your responsibility to take extra care; always use an ashtray, and never empty it into the waste-paper basket.

Many substances are classed as highly inflammable. Always put the cans back into the metal locker provided.

Do not dry clothes on heaters.

Whenever smoke-stop doors are fitted, do not be the one to wedge them open.

It is important to know the procedures in case of fire. If you are not told or shown the escape route, *ask.* All procedures in case of fire have one golden rule - never go back for personal items.

14 *First aid*
Find out where the first-aid room is located, and always report any injury.

Exercise 7

Make up a set of safety rules, either for the building you are in or for your own home.

5.8 Health and safety outside work

As an adult you are now responsible for your own health and safety, and maybe soon that of your family. It is up to you to keep yourself fit and well. In a crisis, however, you may need help.

Exercise 8

Find the correct telephone numbers for the following main services:
a) electricity;
b) gas;
c) water;
d) social services;
e) city engineer (to deal with unsafe buildings, sewer blockages, flooding, ice and snow);
f) your own doctor.

How do you call on the emergency services (fire, police and ambulance)?

The health and social services

Systems of health and social care have now become very complex; it has become increasingly difficult for families to identify even which section of the National Health Service can help them. All the following are part of the country's health and social services:
a) child guidance clinics;
b) the probation service;
c) the community area nursing service;
d) health centres;
e) ante-natal clinics;
f) mental health welfare officers;
g) general practitioners;
h) local-authority housing departments;
i) VD clinics;
j) family clinics.
It is a good idea to find out where these services are to be found in your area; you may not need any of them at present – but the information *may* be useful in the future.

All personal medical services - doctors, dentists, opticians and chemists - are the responsibility of the local Family Practitioner Committee. Where is yours? From its office you can find out how to get on to a doctor's medical list, how to change from one doctor to another and many other things about the health service.

Community services and voluntary organisations

Voluntary organisations offer a great deal of help to the public. They are often manned by trained staff who work free of charge.

One of the best-known is the Samaritans; there is always someone manning the telephone there night and day. They are always ready to listen to problems, and they are in contact with many members of varying professions.

Exercise 9

What is the Samaritans' address and telephone number?

Also find the following useful addresses and telephone numbers:
a) *Family Planning Association* Gives contraceptive advice and counselling. Both males and females can attend.
b) *Brook Advisory Clinic* Gives counselling, advice on contraceptives and abortions to both sexes.
c) *British Pregnancy Advisory Service* Does pregnancy testing without prior consultation with your own doctor.
d) *Citizen's Advice Bureau* Gives help and advice on many subjects, often free of charge. At least once during the week a solicitor is available; you should telephone first to find out when he or she is there.
e) *Marriage Guidance Council.*
f) *Community Relations Council.*
g) *Registrar of Births, Marriages and Deaths.*
h) *Council offices:*
    a) education;
    b) housing;
    c) welfare and mental health.
i) *Department of Health and Social Security.*

5.9 Four important Acts of Parliament

Equal Pay Act 1970 and Sex Discrimination Act 1975

The Equal Pay Act requires employers to give equal pay and conditions to men and women doing the same or very similar work. However, in firms where particular jobs are done entirely by women, pay is still relatively low. The Sex Discrimination Act makes it unlawful to treat anyone less favourably than another person simply on the grounds of sex.

Race Relations Act 1976

This was passed to strengthen the law against racial discrimination. It deals with discrimination on grounds of colour, race, nationality (which includes citizenship) or ethnic or national origins. It defines discrimination in two main ways.
a) *Direct discrimination* consists of treating a person, on racial grounds, less favourably than others are or would be treated in the same circumstances. Segregating a person from others on racial grounds constitutes less favourable treatment.
b) *Indirect discrimination* consists of applying a requirement or condition which, whether intentionally or not, adversely affects one racial group considerably more than another and cannot be justified on non-racial grounds.
At work, this act covers recruitment, terms of employment, training, opportunities for promotion, transfer, etc., and dismissal.

These acts do not apply to private households, or to firms with fewer than five employees - except in cases of victimisation.
  And there are certain fields where employers *may* discriminate on grounds of sex - for example, in some pension schemes where men and women retire at different ages, and in the case of time off because of pregnancy. Also, some positions can only be filled by one sex: for example actor, prison officer, toilet attendant. Add as many more as you can think of.

Exercise 10a

Direct discrimination—two examples
i) Explain in what way these advertisements discriminate.
a) 'Waitress required for busy city centre café'.
b) 'Strong young men wanted for warehouse work'.
ii) Is the following advertisement unlawful? Why - or why not? 'Topless dancer required for city-centre night club'.

Exercise 10b

Indirect discrimination
Give your view of these two advertisements:
i) 'Local publican requires bar staff, preferably attractively dressed in blouse and skirt';
ii) 'Chef required - must be a specialist at preparing haggis'.

Exercise 10c

Similarly it is unlawful to discriminate against a person simply on the grounds of their being single or married, or of a particular religion.

i) Write two advertisements, each showing one of these kinds of discrimination.

ii) Consider the following advertisement and say whether you think it is direct or indirect discrimination, and why.

'Secretary wanted, with plenty of overtime available in a busy department. Not suitable for a person with young children.'

It is also unlawful to victimise a person who has exercised their rights under any of these three acts by, say, giving him or her menial work, offering less overtime or making him or her unfairly redundant.

If you feel you have been discriminated against at work because of your sex you should tell your employer you mean to contact the Equal Opportunities Commission. Similarly, if you feel you have been discriminated against because of your race or colour you should contact the Commission for Racial Equality. If possible, discuss the issue with your boss.

Provided your income and capital are within certain limits you can obtain Legal Aid (financial help with the expenses of a court case) and free legal advice. If you feel this may apply to you, contact

New Legal Aid
PO Box 9
Nottingham NG1 6DS
or, if in Scotland,
Legal Aid Central Committee
PO Box 123
21 Drumslength Gardens
Edinburgh EH3 77R.

If you want information, contact Equal Opportunities Commission, Overseas House, Quay Street, Manchester M3 3HN; Commission for Racial Equality, Elliot House, 10-12 Allington Street, London SW1E 5EH. You can also obtain help and advice from job centres and unemployment benefit offices. Find and write down the addresses and telephone numbers of those nearest or appropriate to you.

Employment Protection Act 1975

This act protects both employer and employee, though in fact it gives more specific rights to the employee. You cannot lose your job just because your employer does not like you, or for similar trivial reasons – though any employer can give you the sack for

a) *incapability:* simple inability to do the job;

b) *misconduct:* stealing, lying, fighting, etc;

c) *redundancy:* your job's ceasing to exist;

d) *contravention of statutory acts:* for example, if you are disqualified from driving you cannot be employed as a driver.

However, you can be dismissed during the first four weeks without reason. After this time your employer must give you *notice* if he intends to dismiss you, and it must be made clear that the dismissal is fair. *Unfair dismissal* can result in a 'reinstatement order' or compensation in cash.

The period of notice (or amount of cash 'in lieu') depends on how long you have been working for the employer concerned. In general terms, after the first four weeks of employment you get one week's notice per year of employment, up to a maximum of twelve weeks.

If, for example, you have been frequently late but no one has grumbled, warned you, or remarked about it, it could be argued that sudden dismissal for continued lateness is unfair dismissal.

Disputes of this kind are settled by *industrial tribunals.* However, the Advisory Conciliation and Arbitration Service may also be brought in. Find out the address and telephone number of this organisation's nearest office.

Exercise 11

a) Comments, please, about the following conversation.

Manager (to industrial tribunal) Yes, I gave Miss Jones her notice of dismissal.

Miss Jones He gave it to me for trying to form a trade-union branch in the factory.

Manager No, that's wrong – I gave her notice for constant shoddy work.

Miss Jones Well, he certainly didn't tell me that was the reason.

Manager But it was. I and others can prove it.

Fair or unfair dismissal?

b) *Milkman* (to dairy manager) I took £25 from the takings last Tuesday, and I put it back on Friday.
Manager Then I'll report you for theft.

The police prosecuted the milkman, who was cleared of theft since he showed he did not intend to keep the money. But later, when dismissed for taking the money, he took the dairy and manager to an industrial tribunal and accused them of unfair dismissal.

Should he have won his case? Comments, please.

Pregnancy

Under this act a woman can no longer be dismissed just because she is pregnant. She is allowed maternity leave, and is entitled to have her job back provided she fulfils certain conditions:
a) she must work until eleven weeks before her baby is due;
b) she must properly inform her employer that she is pregnant but wishes to return to her job;
c) she must return to her job a maximum of twenty-nine weeks after the birth;
d) she must have worked for her employer for two years.
She is entitled to maternity pay for the first six weeks of her absence. The employer gives her nine-tenths of her pay, less any maternity allowance from the government. The employer may take on a temporary replacement, provided it is made properly clear to all concerned that the replacement *is* temporary.

Other rights of employees

a) Employees are entitled to receive, within thirteen weeks of starting in a job, a copy of their contract of employment, giving information on pay, pensions, holidays, working hours, job titles, etc.; and an itemised pay-slip at once.
b) An employee suspended from work on medical grounds will normally be entitled to receive his or her usual wages for up to twenty-six weeks.
c) Certain payments must be made to an employee who is 'laid off' – that is, whose employer cannot find work for him or her to do; but this sometimes depends on the reason for the lay-off.
d) Employees who are union officials are entitled to carry out certain union duties in working hours.
e) Employees who have public duties to perform, for example as magistrates, may be entitled to pay while carrying them out.

What are this woman's rights if, having worked for her employer for three years, she becomes pregnant?

f) An employee who is made redundant is entitled to reasonable time off, with pay, to look for other work or to arrange training for a new job.

For further detailed information on any of this, contact your local office of the Department of Employment whenever it becomes necessary.

5.10 School and work—the differences as some people see them

Copy out the chart below and in the right-hand column write in against each comment what you think would be the difference between being at school and at work.

An employee suspended from work on medical grounds

School	Work
a) School exists for the pupil's benefit.	a)
b) Cannot sack you for being lazy.	b)
c) In school work, a lack of accuracy results in a poor mark.	c)
d) You are used to working with people of your own age, with direction from adults.	d)
e) You may have been a senior pupil, at the top of the school.	e)
f) You are given a good deal of guidance and supervision.	f)
g) At school you are used to a nine-a.m.-to-4 p.m. day with set breaks.	g)
h) Lateness at school may mean a detention or a telling-off.	h)
i) The school day is divided up into varying activities —those of the brain, physical activities (sport) and practical work.	i)

Whatever the differences you encounter between school and work, a pleasant manner, hard work, and a willingness to learn and do the 'menial' tasks sometimes demanded of a beginner, will, as at school, stand you in good stead.

5.11 Some questions
This unit should have enabled you to answer the following questions.

1 What promises does an employer make to an employee, and what are the responsibilities of the employee to the employer?

2 What information would you expect to find
a) on a wage slip?
b) on a form P60?

3 What benefits do you and your family get from the money deducted from your wages for income tax and National Insurance contributions? Do you think these benefits are worth such deductions? (It may be interesting to find out how much is paid by your whole family in contributions before you discuss this question - and also how frequently you and your family need to make use of the services concerned.)

4 What would you say to a foreign visitor who came to this country with the intention of using our 'free' medical services for treatment which he or she could either not afford or not obtain at home?

5 What arguments would you use in trying to persuade a colleague to join a trade union? What reasons do you think he or she might give for not wishing to do so?

6 Give five simple rules about health and safety which could be usefully applied a) at home, b) at work, and c) in a youth club.

7 In what ways could you help a colleague who believed he or she was not getting a fair deal because he or she was the 'wrong' sex, or the 'wrong' race?

Unit 6 **Equal opportunities?**

It is sometimes said that laws always follow events. (Consider for interest the most recent laws on abortion and homosexuality.) But for many years most people have acknowledged that equality of opportunity is right – and although this has brought about, among other things, comprehensive schools and the abolition of selection of pupils at 11 +, it has not resulted in schools' giving an equal chance to all their pupils, or in tutors' attaching equal importance to the development of all their students.

Such thinking can upset very old and firmly held views and prejudices against women playing the same roles as or having equal responsibility with men. For instance, although Lenin said that 'Every cook must learn to rule the state', very few women are members of the Supreme Soviet, the equivalent of our House of Commons. And the law providing for equality was passed more than fifty years ago in the USSR, in contrast to this country. Laws can never become fully implemented and effective until they affect people's thinking and attitudes.

This unit is intended to help you to understand the issues involved, and to recognise what your own attitudes are and what prejudices you may still hold about real equality of boys and girls, men and women. It is hoped the unit will enable you to determine what kind of relationship you want with the opposite sex – and whether, if you are a girl, you want to share the responsibilities of partnership or, as in the past, be dependent upon and basically of secondary importance to a man. Your attitudes will be apparent to others from what you do and say, and will affect the way in which your children are brought up. As far as boys and men are concerned, swallowing their pride may be their most difficult problem; but they should remember that equality implies that
a) punishment for wrong-doing is equally administered;
b) wives and girlfriends share the bills;
c) all the ways in which boys have thought that girls 'get away with it' are vanishing or may soon vanish.

6.1 Men, women or persons?
During the last war women drove heavy lorries, flew aircraft across the Atlantic, fought fires, served on gunsites and parachuted behind enemy lines. Do you think that women as well as men *should* carry out such tasks?

Exercise 1

Some people argue that the apparent difference of interest between boys and girls stems from their treatment by parents at a very early age.

Name six toys you would buy for a six-year-old girl. Name six toys you would buy for a six-year-old boy. Would either get the same pleasure from the other's toys? Do you think toys give children a picture of themselves? *Should* different toys be given to children of different sexes? Would girls like (or do they like) chemistry-sets or train-sets? – or skateboards?

It has been said that girls stop playing with toys when they are about nine years old, but boys and men play with toys all their lives. Do you think this is true? Why? Consider engines, boats and trains as toys, and compare them with what one thinks of as girls' toys.

What toys would you choose for your own children? Would you expect both your sons and your daughters to sew on buttons, wash dishes, dig the garden, climb trees, organise parties and cook food? Explain your reasons.

What changes in the treatment of boys, girls, men and women would you like to see
a) at home
b) at school
c) at work
in the next ten years?

What do you think of the following newspaper items? Comments, please!

The strong man they call Maria

The interpreter pointed to a sad-eyed, short-cropped, track-suited figure. 'He is our star player. Like, whataya call 'im . . . Trevor Francis?' Then with pride he pointed to a burlier track-suited female: 'And he is the only woman metalworker in Italy. He plays in defence at no. 2.'

It was, I confess, all a little confusing meeting the seventeen Italian women footballers who are here to play England's women at Wimbledon tonight in what is building up nicely into a bit of a needle international as a prelude to tomorrow's all-male battle at Wembley.

The ladies of Italy were doing just what any of their male counterparts would be doing while filling in time between a training session and lunch at London's Crystal Palace. They were playing cards.

A couple were trying their hands at darts and giving pretty good impersonations of whale-hunters trying to get a harpoon into Moby Dick.

Their manager is Amadeo Amadei who played centre-forward for Italy when England beat them 2 —0 at Tottenham in 1949 and scored for them in the 1 —1 draw at Florence three years ago.

He knows all about us, especially after a six-year spell with Napoli at a time when they lorded it over the Italian first division.

He says there are between seven and eight thousand women footballers in Italy and that his national squad is just about as good as any in Europe.

Exploding the male myth

Dear Sir,

When researching for male and female athletic comparisons, Liz Ferris ('Exploding the Male Myth') overlooked a living example of women outperforming men. I refer to Beryl Burton (Morley Cycle Club) who, in 1967, broke the women's national record for a 12-hour time trial, covering 277.25 miles. In the same event M. McNamara (Rockingham CC) established a new men's record of 276.52 miles.

In events open to both men and women, Mrs Burton has on a number of occasions beaten all comers, and her best performances compare favourably with current men's records: 10 miles —21 min. 25 sec. (20 min. 27 sec. for men); 25 miles —53 min. 21 sec. (51 min.); 50 miles —1 hr 51 min. 30 sec. (1 hr. 43 min. 46 sec.); 100 miles —3 hr 55 min. 5 sec. (3 hr 46 min. 22 sec.).

Mrs Burton has dominated women's cycling for nineteen years and must be acknowledged as an extraordinary athlete. However, the number of female racing cyclists compared with male competitors is sadly very low, otherwise, given the same ratios that occur in swimming and athletics, there would be other revelations to lend support to Miss Ferris's theories.

Queen of the extraloo

All change at the ladies as Ann becomes a train driver
The penny has at last dropped on London's tube

Yesterday the District Line became the Extraloo Line.

It was all because of thirty-six-year-old Mrs Ann Dadds —Britain's first woman train-driver.

Until now, only the lack of a ladies at Underground depots has held back the promotion of women into tube-train cabs.

That has been put right. So Mrs Dadds led the way into a little bit of history yesterday.

'Most of the toilets were planned with men in mind. It has taken several years for us to be in a position to take women drivers,' said a London Transport spokesman.

Ann, married to a police dog-handler, said: 'I am looking forward to the job tremendously.

'I particularly enjoy getting on with a job on my own, which you get as a driver.

'You always get some ribbing over something like this from your male colleagues but I give back as good as I get.

'I am not particularly a women's lib fan, but it's rubbish what a lot of men say about women drivers. Most of them are very good.'

Ann, of Plaistow, east London, said she had not met a single 'male chauvinist' during her training.

Many passengers had been surprised to see a woman in the cab and children had waved to her.

'We believe Mrs Dadds is the first woman in Britain to qualify to drive a train,' said the LT spokesman.

'For the past seven months she has been a guard or driver on the District Line in a post known as a motorman. We may have to reconsider the job title.'

Ann has worked for LT for nine years and now steps up to an average weekly wage of £100, the same as the men.

So now it can be the dream of all little girls to be a train-driver.

The problems of a pregnant Marine

Quantico, Virginia

A woman five and a half months pregnant is nearing the end of a tough twenty-one-week officer training course at the Quantico Marine Corps base.

Laurie Glenn Jacobson has marched miles across rugged terrain with a helmet, seven-pound rifle and a 25 lb pack.

Second Lieutenant Mrs Jacobson, five foot tall and weighing 8½ stone, has shouldered a machine-gun tripod and four hundred rounds of ammunition during a field exercise.

The only exercise she has not fully taken part in was a three-day simulated war involving tear gas.

'The doctor told me not to take aspirin, so I thought tear gas would be a bad idea,' she explained.

Mrs Jacobson , twenty-five, is one of the first pregnant women to undergo the rigours of Marine Corps training. Until a year ago only men went through it.

Wife of a Marine first lieutenant stationed on Okinawa, Mrs Jacobson is one of fifteen women in the 244-person Charlie Company, and the only one who is pregnant.

Marine officials said that of the five thousand women in the corps today, forty-four are pregnant and have chosen to stay on active duty. And with ten thousand women expected in the Marines' ranks by 1985, headquarters is at work on a Marine maternity uniform.

Until July 1975 women Marines who became pregnant were automatically discharged. Now official Marine policy is to leave the matter up to the woman and her doctor.

'I believe my body will let me know when I'm doing something I shouldn't,' said Mrs Jacobson.

90

6.2 Men and women at work

The most important recent changes in British working life have concerned the position of women. More and more women are working after – or while – raising a family. But real hard-line 'women's libbers' are still quite rare. According to several women's magazines, most women still like to be thought attractive and want their male partners to be courteous and considerate. If that is so, it will take many years for genuine equality to arrive. Applications from men who want to be shorthand typists and women who want to be train-drivers will not flood in for some years to come.

But what about other countries? In the USSR there are five times as many women doctors and scientists as in Britain, and fifteen times as many women engineers. Why do you think this is so? Are Russian women more ambitious, more disciplined, more strongly directed to jobs? Do British women have less opportunity and less drive? What do you think?

Exercise 2

More boys than girls in Britain sit five O-levels or more, but girls on average pass their O-levels with higher marks. Are boys

more ambitious than girls? Are they less clever, or just lazier?

Women on average live longer than men. Can you think of anything in the different life-styles of men and women or any other factors that might account for this? In view of this, how can you justify their retirement at an earlier age?

Traditionally, in this country, the man has been the breadwinner, going out to work to earn money to keep his wife and family. His wife has brought up the children and looked after the home. How have the situations and attitudes of men and women changed? Do you think this is better than the traditional life? Why? Has it been a necessary or a voluntary change? Give reasons for your views.

It is often claimed that, weight for weight, a man is stronger than a woman, but that women can do some things better than men can, such as work requiring fine finger-movements. Can you think of other alleged differences? Are these real?

Exercise 3   Who does what?

Make a list of jobs you think can *only* be done by men, and a second list of jobs that can *only* be done by women.

Give six examples of traditional men's jobs which are attracting more and more women as the years go by. Can you think of any 'women's' jobs which are attracting more men?

Why do you think that there are no female miners in this country and only a very few male midwives? Do men make as good nurses as women? Certainly the men are outnumbered. Why do you think this is? Men far outnumber women on many assembly lines. Why? Does shift work have any effect on this?

Why do married women go to work?
a) Of necessity, to make sure the family has enough income?
b) To relieve boredom?
c) To meet new friends?
d) To have enough money to be independent?
e) To get out of the house and away from housework?

Weight for weight men are usually stronger than women, but what is strength?

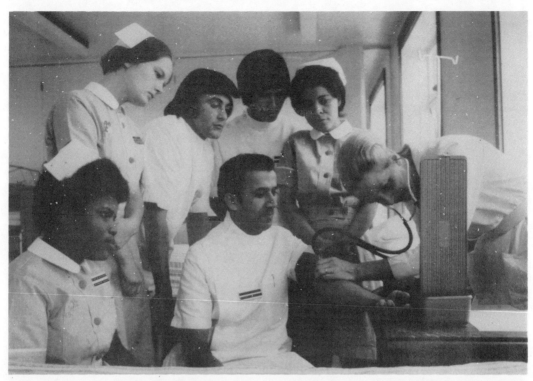

Some more examples of reversed roles

f) Because they are interested in their work?

Ask six women what job they do and why they go to work. Explain what you are doing first and, if they tell you to mind your own business, ask others. Try to choose women from different groups – single women, working wives, single-parent families and so on – so you can see how their answers compare. Then ask six men.

Exercise 4 'Top jobs'

Think of a number of important jobs: doctor, builder, bank manager, bishop, judge, general, government minister and so on. Try to name as many women as you can in each category. Why do you think you get the kind of answers you do? Are there opportunities for women to do these jobs? Do women have equal opportunities for promotion to top jobs at work? Ask around your parents and friends.

Why do you think that, despite the Equal Pay Act, jobs done and businesses staffed mainly by women still pay low wages? What would happen if men applied? Do you think men *would* apply? Why, or why not?

Another thing about the Equal Pay Act is that women are exposed to more danger as a result of it. For example, policewomen are now just as likely as policemen to be sent to a nasty trouble-spot if they happen to be nearer to it. In the USA, women are being considered as front-line troops. In Israel and many other countries women already fight alongside men. Do you think they should?

Did you hear the story of Sally, aged five, who had just started school? Her infant teacher was a young man, whom everyone on the staff liked very much. When, after a fortnight or so, Sally's mother asked, 'What's your teacher like?', Sally replied, 'I don't know, mummy, she's only sent her husband so far.'

Perhaps you would like to discuss this. Do women make better infant teachers

Men's lib?

than men? Why do you feel the way you do about this?

Exercise 5

Finally, imagine that you are the local leader of a men's liberation movement. What would you suggest it might agitate to achieve?

6.3 Some questions

It is hoped that this unit has enabled you to answer thoughtfully the following questions.

1   What benefits have resulted or will result from the belief that boys and girls should have equal opportunities and responsibilities?

2   What advantages or disadvantages have you found in being a boy or a girl? (The author would like to know your answer.)

3   How, in your view, would equality change family life?

4   What arguments might a girl use to an employer who did not wish to give her employment, training or promotion because she was likely to get married in the near future?

5   In bringing up children, are mothers more important than fathers, or are both needed to ensure the best kind of upbringing and the best chances?
6   What advice would you give to a girl who wanted to become
a) a technician;
b) a train driver;
c) a surgeon?
And to a boy who wanted to become
a) an infant teacher;
b) a midwife;
c) a beautician?